FROME
4/14

Please return/renew this item by the last date shown on this label, or on your self-service receipt.

To renew this item, visit **www.librarieswest.org.uk** or contact your library

Your borrower number and PIN are required.

1 3 1523254 2

JUST A JOB IN BURUNDI

Judith Brown

MINERVA PRESS
MONTREUX   LONDON   WASHINGTON

JUST A JOB IN BURUNDI
Copyright © Judith Brown 1996

ISBN 1 86106 099 8

First Published 1996 by
MINERVA PRESS
195 Knightsbridge
London SW7 1RE

Printed in Great Britain by
B.W.D. Ltd, Northolt, Middlesex

JUST A JOB IN BURUNDI

Contents

Preface

Between February and May 1995, Judith Brown went to work in a refugee camp in Burundi, first as a nurse, and then as a Health Coordinator for CONCERN WORLDWIDE.

She left behind her husband and three children for an exciting adventure in Africa. Whilst she was in Burundi, civil unrest broke out and hundreds of people were massacred. This was widely reported in the news at home, although her family were unable to get news of her as most of the time she was four hours away from a telephone line.

This is a story of her understanding of the Burundian and Rwandan conflict, combined with the routine and pressures of her life working in the camp, the stresses of her family while she was away, and the reflections of the usefulness of her work after she returned.

The Call

I had been waiting for a year. In the middle of February 1995 I got the phone call I had wanted.

"We need a nurse in Burundi."

I didn't know where Burundi was or what I had to do. I said immediately I would go.

History And Violence

The past, present and future of Burundi cannot be described without reference to its close neighbour, Rwanda, which shares its legacy of ethnic and racial tension and conflict. Inevitably, the account will be dominated by the relationship between two tribes, the Watutsi (or Tutsi) and the Hutu.

When I went to northern Burundi to work in early 1995, my task was to look after the health needs of 27,000 Rwandan Hutu refugees who were accommodated in a camp in the northern province of Kirundo. Like many others before me, I became confused, as I could not easily identify differences between tribal characteristics to account for the hatred and brutality, which some people have described as the worst ever in the world's history. The search for an answer made me intrigued about the cause of the conflict, but less able to define a way forward to prevent yet further destruction of life.

It might be tempting for an outsider to think that the waste of life and terrible fear engendered throughout the whole population was pointless. Researching the issue revealed a complicated web of answers which, in themselves, asked more questions, but the genocidal killing and torture which is the common heritage of every Burundian and Rwandan is far from being without reason or cause. The Tutsi and Hutu, Burundian and Rwandan, treat visitors from overseas with gentility and courtesy, they are a people who seem content to have very little and who are at ease with themselves. The country appears at first view to be a serene and fertile idyllic rural paradise. And yet, beneath the apparent peace and balance, Burundi hides its volatile and unpredictable nature. Its past has demonstrated that at any moment, from this utopian serenity, often without an obvious reason for the dramatic change, an awful, unrespecting, bloody and brutal violence can emerge to dramatically change or end the life of an individual, a family, a village or a tribe. And from this often unexpected bloodletting, no person who lives or visits the area can consider themselves immune.

Burundi and Rwanda form a shape a bit like an egg, with Rwanda in the north and Burundi in the south. They are small countries, each occupying an area about the size of Wales. They are situated in the middle of Africa, just south of the equator, landlocked, bounded on the north by Uganda, in the east by Zaire, in the south and west by Tanzania. They are divided along most of their borders by rivers and lakes.

Unlike most African countries, Burundi and Rwanda were not absorbed into larger political entities, and retained their identities and traditional borders, although they were administered jointly by Belgium as a League of Nations Protectorate. Historically they were the kingdoms of Urundi and Ruanda and were almost invariably enemies, and traditional rivalry remains strong.

The first inhabitants of Rwanda and Burundi were the Twa, who were hunters and gatherers. Somewhere between the 4th and 7th centuries, a collection of Bantu clans known as Hutu settled in the area and they appear to have been agriculturalists. The Tutsi tribes arrived later and their origins are subject to much debate, but they are traditionally held to be pastoralists, perhaps originating from Ethiopia. Although the origins are debated, it is known that the Tutsi learned the Hutu language, Kirundi, and that from the outset the clans intermarried.

Burundi was ruled via a monarchy which began with Mwami [king] Ntare I in the 17th century. In Rwanda, power became centralised and dominated by the Tutsi monarchy, and the lower classes were Hutu. This did not happen in Burundi because of an intermediate ruling class known as the *ganwa*, who were mainly from the Tutsi tribe. The presence of the *ganwa* meant that there was not such obvious ethnic polarity. As there was a middle group there was more intermarriage and more fluidity in moving from one tribe to another.

Relationships between the Hutu and ordinary Tutsi were on an equal footing. There were two clans of Tutsi, the Batare and the Bezi, and when the ruling monarch died, there was frequently bloodshed between the two groups in order to decide the succession. Ethnic tension was traditionally between these two Tutsi groups, whilst ordinary Hutu and Tutsi lived peacefully alongside each other.

Although the Tutsi have dominated the monarchy since the 17th century, they are not the largest tribe. The ethnic composition of Burundi is generally held to be about 85% Hutu, 14% Tutsi, and 1% Twa. This tribal mix was what was found by the German imperialists who arrived in Burundi in 1899, and after initial aggression, the Tutsi monarch King Ntare II provided support for them. He was a Bezi and because of this clan's acceptance of the new rulers, they retained their hold on the monarchy. This was still the case when the Belgians assumed control of Burundi in 1919, together with its neighbour Rwanda, as a League of Nations mandated territory called Ruanda-Urundi. The Belgians did not rule directly, but instead used the *ganwa* in Burundi as tax collectors and leviers and appeal judges. They also expected the *ganwa* to organise forced labour for developing the infrastructure and for growing coffee. This favouring of Tutsi, and in particular the Bezi, increased ethnic polarisation and interfered with the previous balance between the tribes.

After 1948, the Belgians, under direction from the UN, moved towards some degree of democratisation. The Belgians used delaying tactics over granting independence. In 1957 a decision by the United Nations (UN) to visit Burundi galvanised political activity. This meant that local political parties started to form, and many of these were divided by tribal alliances.

One of the main parties which emerged was Uprona, which stood for *Union pour le Progress National*, which was formed by a *ganwa* called Bihumugani. Eventually, a son of the king called Prince Rwagasore assumed control of Uprona in 1958 and demanded immediate independence. He managed to offend the Belgian administration whilst attracting support from a range of tribes, including rural Hutu, Bezi *ganwa* and the small number of people who worked in towns. The Belgians' distaste for Rwagasore led them to support an alternative party, the *Partie Democratique Chretien* (PDC) led by Biroli. This was a party which had support of an urban élite and the Batare, who were the historical adversaries of the Bezi.

The path to independence continued, and in 1959, internal autonomy was granted as a precursor to full independence. Uprona won elections comfortably and also went on to successfully contest the communal and legislative elections two years later. It is generally felt that the complex character of Rwagasore was a unifying force as he had a wide range of followers from different tribes. His assassination two weeks after the elections could therefore be considered a crucial event in Burundi's history, as Uprona became divided and ethnically polarised, and for the first time, open conflict between Hutu and Tutsi emerged. Independence was granted in 1962, and Rwagasore's father, King Mwambutsa, exploited the vacuum left by the death of his son by taking over control and he appointed Uprona's founder, Bihumugani, as prime minister. Bihumugani was a Bezi Tutsi and he placed members of his tribe and family into key posts.

Until independence, Burundi and Rwanda were still one joint protectorate, but in 1963 Rwanda formally broke with Burundi, and Burundi became a country recognised in its own right. The *mwami*, King Mwambutsa, wanted to consolidate his own position and therefore he tried to ensure that there was a balance of Tutsi and Hutu in government so that he had wider support. Between 1962 and 1965 the unstable situation produced four governments, and yet again in 1965 a prime minister was killed, this time a Hutu called Ngendandumwe, who was killed one week after taking office.

Meanwhile, events in Rwanda were also dominated by ethnic differences, and there, Hutu were blamed for terrible violent uprisings with Tutsi suffering most of the persecution. Many Tutsi fled, and an estimated 300,000 refugees mostly headed for Burundi. The widespread anti-Tutsi violence by Hutu rulers in Rwanda made the Tutsi rulers in Burundi feel particularly threatened. After Ngendandumwe was assassinated, there were new elections. By now political parties were polarised, and because of the Hutu majority in the population, not surprisingly, Hutu political parties were returned with a decisive victory. Nonetheless, the Tutsi king, perhaps fearing that the events in Rwanda would be repeated in Burundi, appointed a Tutsi as prime minister. This enraged the Hutu, and an attempted *coup-d'état* ensued but it was not successful. The repression of this coup attempt was extremely violent. Fearing the Hutu, the Tutsi dominated army selectively killed any educated or politically interested Hutu and any of their followers, which meant that Hutu did not participate in political life for many years. In the tense situation which resulted, the king was deposed by his son, who in turn was deposed by his prime minister, a Tutsi called Micombero, who ended the monarchy and declared Burundi to be a republic in 1966.

The end of the Tutsi dominated monarchy, however, did not lead to any alteration in the overwhelming Tutsi control of the army, politics, commercial life and educational institutions in Burundi, and with the abolition of the monarchy, a stabilising political influence was removed. Hutus were frustrated at their inability to take power by democratic means and this inevitably led to coup attempts. Tutsi massacres and purges continued, and after yet another unsuccessful Hutu coup in 1972, the army inflicted its terrible revenge with up to two hundred thousand Hutu killed and the same number fleeing the country.

This set the pattern for Burundian politics, with each group fearful and untrusting of the other. Politicians who came to power were inevitably Tutsi, and although initially some of them held moderate or conciliatory viewpoints, this seemed to be altered by experience and ended in the same polarisation and fearful control. The norm for a change of government seemed to be by coup rather than election, although there were one-candidate elections in 1984 with universal suffrage, where the then prime minister, Bagaza of the Uprona party, received over 99% of the vote. Meanwhile, the world watched as the numbers of political prisoners increased and acts of torture were reported.

Bagaza was deposed by *coup d'état* in 1987 by Buyoya, who dissolved Uprona and suspended the constitution, but nothing much changed. Further large-scale uprisings of Hutu in the north of Burundi were put down by Tutsi armies in 1989, leading to yet more Hutu refugees fleeing from Burundi. This became a turning point when Tutsi leaders realised that they could no longer hold back the Hutu demand for recognition and political representation. In October, Buyoya announced the appointment of a Hutu as prime minister and political bodies started to appear more representative of the ethnic divide, with both Hutu and Tutsi in equal numbers. Even so, the suspicion on both sides meant that this did not reduce the claims and counterclaims of atrocities which were frequently voiced and often substantiated by each side of the ethnic divide.

By 1990, a charter of national unity and a programme of political reform was announced, with a new constitution and freedom to start any ethnically mixed political party, and this led to elections in 1993. A predominantly Hutu party called Frodebu, *Front pour la democratic au Burundi*, won a substantial victory, and for the first time in over four hundred years, a Hutu, Melchior Ndadye, wielded supreme power in Burundi. Ndadye had a forty-six point plan which aimed to rid Burundi of its 'ethnic disease'. He began the healing process and reform of the military and civil service, and in doing so upset the hard-liners who saw the privileges which they had accrued under threat. One hundred days after his election, Ndadye was brutally murdered by a section of his own mainly Tutsi army. This led to further Hutu uprisings and the usual Tutsi repression. At the same time that Ndadye was assassinated, many people who had links to Frodebu who held similar views were also killed, together with their wives.

Amazingly, the rebellion was ended after appeals from the Tutsi prime minister, who had been elected by Ndadye, and the coup was defeated. Cyprien Ntarymamira was elected president and until his death presided over a coalition of Frodebu and Uprona. He was killed along with the Rwandan president Habyarimana in Kigali in April 1994, when the plane in which they were travelling was shot down. Whilst this resulted in chaos and unprecedented violence and genocide in Rwanda, in Burundi the after-effects were more subdued. But since then, episodes of ethnic tension have constantly risen to the surface with sporadic outbursts of killings and reprisals.

Over this tense situation the latest president, Sylvestre Ntibantunganya, ruled an uneasy country wherein Hutu still felt resentful, despite their recent political successes, and fearful of the Tutsi dominated army, civil service and educational institutions. In his words there appeared desperation in the search for a way of uniting this distrustful, traumatised and fearfully divided nation: "How long is blood going to flow in this country? What do you gain from killing and shedding blood? Can you drink it? Build houses from it? You must live together – I come with a present of justice, unity and peace."

How Rwandan Refugees Arrived In Burundi

In 1945, the world witnessed the dropping of the first atomic bombs in Hiroshima and Nagasaki. Two hundred thousand people were killed in these awful events – enough to shock the world at its power, and stop the usage, but not the development, of nuclear weaponry. From the moment that the world became aware of the power of destruction it held at its fingertips, countries have resisted finding a need to repeat the massacre of hundreds of civilians which included women and children.

This point is described in order to put into perspective just how terrible were the events which started in April 1994 in the small country of Rwanda. It is estimated that 500,000 to 900,000 people, mainly civilians, and including women and children, were massacred, by machete. The world watched but did not act, as horrific events unfolded. So far the world has found no solution to guarantee peace and trust in Rwanda and Burundi, which both still hold the potential for brutality on a massive scale.

Rwanda, like Burundi, is beautiful. It is sometimes called *Les Milles Collines* – the thousand hills. It is not spectacular or awesome, but lush, green and cultivated over most of its sloping landscape, reddish-brown huts surrounded by banana palms are dotted amongst its hills, with lakes and rivers running along its valleys. Until the genocide of 1994, it was a country which supported a population of three hundred people per square mile, the majority of whom were subsistence farmers living off their land. It was in this rural setting that hundreds of thousands were massacred, and it was from here that millions of others fled to the neighbouring lands of Zaire, Tanzania, and Burundi. The story cannot be complete unless it tries to describe why these Rwandans left their homes and land, gave up their livelihood, and came to settle in Ruku camp in the Kirundo province of northern Burundi as refugees in a hostile country.

The same ethnic mix exists in Rwanda as in Burundi, but estimates relating to the proportion of Tutsi and Hutu vary. Because Tutsi have been persecuted, killed and driven out of Rwanda, some sources calculate that the proportion of Tutsi is now between four and nine percent, with the Hutu majority reaching up to ninety-five percent.

The development of the Rwandan social structure had evolved in a different way from Burundi, because they did not have the intermediate class, the *ganwa*. Instead, since the 15th century, the Tutsi dominated a very subservient Hutu population, often ensuring domination by brutal and repressive means. Over the years the relations between tribes reached a stage where the divisions were starting to become more of a class difference and intermarriage became possible. This unification of tribes was upset by the arrival of colonial powers who gave extra rights and privileges to the Tutsi, the differences became more distinct, and the seeds of resentment flourished once more.

The infrastructure of Rwanda was organised by forced labour. Instead of paying taxes, people of Rwanda were obliged to work one day each week doing tasks such as building roads and schools. This "forced labour" was organised by a group called the *interahamwe*. This group, agents of the government, could also be used to spread propaganda by the government in power.

When Rwanda reached independence, instead of the Tutsi holding on to a dominant position, as occurred in Burundi, the Hutu were determined that they would no longer be subservient. As independence approached, violence increased. The Hutu cause was supported by Belgium and they decisively won the first election in 1962. During the next three years it is estimated that more than half of the Tutsi population were massacred by resentful Hutu whilst the Hutu government did nothing to intervene. Large numbers of Tutsi were displaced to Uganda and Burundi. In Burundi, many settled in the capital of Bujumbura, where many found work in white collar occupations in a political climate which favoured their ethnic group. Meanwhile, the Hutu remained in control of Rwanda, and in 1973, following a successful coup, President Habyarimana, a Hutu from the north of Rwanda, seized power, which he retained until his assassination in 1994. No doubt the Hutu rulers in Rwanda felt the same apprehension and unease when looking over their shoulders at the example set in Burundi, which fuelled their fear of allowing Tutsi to be involved in government and political processes.

The Rwandese, who had left their homeland and settled elsewhere, were known as Banyarwanda, which means they are speakers of Kinyarwanda, the native language of Rwanda. The Banyarwanda who had settled in Uganda were never fully accepted, and from time to time were harassed and driven from their lands. Many of them were young, well-educated, and had acquired military training in the Ugandan resistance army. They called themselves the Rwandan Patriotic Front (RPF) and posed a threat to the security of Rwanda.

In October 1990, Rwanda was invaded from the north by the RPF, who occupied several towns before the Rwandan army joined forces with Zairean troops to turn back the RPF before it arrived at Kigali. The RPF consisted of not only Tutsi, but also disaffected Hutu who were opposed to Habyarimana's regime. To the international community, the RPF invaders were seen as a democratic multi-ethnic group who wanted to depose a corrupt government. During 1991 and 1992, Habyarimana was increasingly accused of violating human rights, not only of Tutsi, but also of the Hutu, who lived in the south of Rwanda and who had voiced opposition to his rule. The repeated border incursions from the RPF in the north and the human rights violations led to more displaced Rwandans fleeing their homeland over the next few years. Meanwhile, the Hutu supporters of Habyarimana were indoctrinated with anti-Tutsi hatred, and the presence of death lists held by his supporters were well-known, to the extent that it was possible to pay to have your name removed from the list. All tribes were finding more reasons to fear the opposing ethnic group.

One of the reasons for the increasing distrust was the quickly deteriorating economy of Rwanda. In 1989, the world coffee prices collapsed. Coffee was the main earner of foreign currency for Rwanda and Burundi, and so this had a profound effect on the already fragile economy of the region. The fast growing population found that there were fewer jobs, less money, and that overpopulation ensured there were fewer farms to hand down from family to family. The overfarmed lands were becoming increasingly less fertile. Thus all of the traditional methods of employment disappeared and food was short. Further problems occurred when the World Bank became involved in supporting the collapsing economy. Strict controls of already limited public spending were introduced, reducing the possibility of education and health care. A disenchanted, bored, and hungry population was constantly told by the *interahamwe* (representatives of the government) that the lack of employment opportunities was because the Tutsi had not been annihilated in the last uprising. Meanwhile, educated Tutsi were denied employment and public office under rules laid down by Habyarimana; instead they turned their hand to business, and some of them did well, thus giving credibility to the *interahamwe* claim.

In order to try to improve his international credibility and prevent further military incursions, Habyarimana was forced to negotiate with the RPF. Lengthy discussions took place in Arusha, Tanzania, which were intended to settle the refugee question once and for all by fostering a climate in which refugees could return. Up to this point the president had resisted all efforts to allow refugees to return, saying that the country was too full to take any more. The talks, called the Arusha Accords, were supported by the Organisation of African Unity (OAU), Rwanda's neighbours, and four northern observer countries – Belgium, France, Germany and USA. This was at odds with the reports of human rights abuses which continued to come from Rwanda, and it is hard to understand why so many countries – including USA, France and South Africa – continued to supply arms to Habyarimana's regime. Despite a declining economic position, Rwanda's army and military equipment was rapidly growing. The political reforms agreed by Habyarimana were not instituted due to his skilful use of a 'divide and rule' policy, which meant the opposition parties were unable to agree a way in which to implement them. The UN were fully aware of all of the tensions in Rwandan life, and the United Nations Assistance Mission to Rwanda (UNAMIR) had sent 2,539 personnel to oversee the peace process following the Arusha Accords agreement in October 1993.

On 6th April 1994, an aircraft carrying the presidents of Burundi and Rwanda was shot down at Kigali as it was coming in to land on return from talks in Arusha. Everyone on board was killed. Although Belgian UN troops were accused by the Rwandese government, it seems more likely that it was shot down by forces of organisations who were intent on sabotaging the Arusha Accords. Road blocks were instantly set up by militiamen and identity cards checked. Any Tutsi, as well as all members of the opposition parties or human rights activists, were set upon by machetes. By April 8th, hundreds of Tutsi civilians and many politicians were killed, including many moderate Hutu who had opposed the corrupt rule of Habyarimana.

The UN forces were much criticised for rescuing foreigners, but not protecting Rwandese in the ensuing bloodbath. In fact they withdrew forces and had a very limited mandate to help with humanitarian aid and to monitor developments. Under these circumstances, the militia were able to continue their campaign of genocide unopposed, which proceeded with ruthless efficiency.

The RPF took advantage of the situation and advanced from the north, meeting little resistance from the Rwandese interim government forces who were ill-disciplined, poorly motivated, and unused to fighting. But the RPF could not match the pace of the militia who were massacring the civilian population. The defenceless Tutsi and moderate Hutu population were killed with machete and iron bars, many pleading to be shot rather than being hacked to death. Victims were slaughtered in every situation, including hospitals and churches, in village after village, region after region. The frenzy of killing meant that people murdered others they had known all of their lives, as they believed that to ensure the survival of the Hutu meant that all Tutsi had to be physically eliminated, and if they did not join in the killing then they themselves were seen as collaborators and would become victims.

Some communities such as Butare in the south of Rwanda enjoyed very peaceful relationships with their ethnic neighbours and initially the population as a whole resisted the orders to kill for some weeks. But more and more pressure from those outside the area eventually forced Hutu to kill Tutsi. Any Hutu who hid a Tutsi wife, family member or friend was likely to be killed himself, and many paid the ultimate price of loyalty with their lives. The *interahamwe* wanted all Hutu to have blood on their hands. Only in this way did they feel safe from any possible recriminations which might occur later.

Personal accounts include stories such as Hutu men who were forced to kill their Tutsi wife, knowing that otherwise they and all of their children would be killed as well. There were many stories of people being killed in churches. The *interahamwe* would make holes in the church wall and throw in grenades. One such account was from a Rwandan woman who was sheltering in a church with her four-year-old son. The grenades and shooting through the church wall killed most of the people sheltering there. She was saved by the corpses of the dead which landed on her. When the militia went away, she hunted for her son and found him dying from a head wound. She carried him outside, cradling him in her arms. As she got outside, a group of men warned her that the militia were returning. She could not flee with her dying son in her arms. So she put him on the church steps to die alone and ran away. There are many other equally heart-rending accounts of the suffering of individuals and families which demonstrate the devastating effect on the lives of most ordinary Rwandese at this time.

As the RPF with its Tutsi dominance advanced from the north during April and May, tens of thousands of Hutu fled in panic before them, believing government propaganda in which they had been repeatedly told that the rebels were intent on killing them. It was the fastest flow of refugees that the world had ever witnessed. Estimates vary, but it is probable that at least 1½ million fled to Zaire, a million to Tanzania, and a quarter of a million to Burundi. This was a catastrophe unprecedented in Africa, a continent used to warfare and disaster. Amongst those who were forced to flee with the advance of the RPF were the innocent and vulnerable who had witnessed scenes of killing of their friends and family members the horror of which we can hardly imagine. Also there were the militia who were themselves the perpetrators of crimes who are waiting for their chance to return to attack the tribe that history has demonstrated to be an unforgiving and unpredictable enemy. Innocent or guilty, they are a people who have resisted all efforts to repatriate them in their homeland. Some have settled into an existence as a refugee in Burundi, a hostile country which did not welcome them and does not want them. These were the people that I was to meet and work with in the Rukuramigabo Camp in Burundi.

Non-Government Organisations – What They Are And What They Are Not

When I went to work in Burundi my new employer was CONCERN WORLDWIDE, an Irish Organisation which began its work in response to the Biafran disaster of 1968. Since then it has specialised in disaster relief but also it has become involved in development, and so this too has become an important part of CONCERN's activities. CONCERN states that it is committed to offering assistance to people who are amongst the poorest in the world. Its function is to offer relief aid and development aid, and as an organisation it aims not to involve itself in political or religious activities but to concentrate on delivering humanitarian support.

Some organisations, such as African Rights in 1994, not only question whether non-governmental organisations (NGO) like CONCERN can be non-political but also ask whether a strictly non-political stance, if it was possible, is the best way of responding to a situation. African Rights claim that NGO have increasingly become more political in complex emergencies in Africa. It claims they are significant political actors and have expanded their mandate to encompass human rights and conflict resolution. Relief agencies are increasingly empowered to make important political judgments which go far beyond their traditional role.

Until the end of the eighties, the world for humanitarian organisations was relatively simple, because the American and Russian superpowers competed for influence, and with centralised control this restricted the activities of relief agencies. In order to work in a country, the consent and cooperation of the government concerned had to be obtained. Relief agencies and western governments acknowledged the right of host governments to expel international agencies which did not keep to the rules. This made NGOs silent witnesses to many atrocities. Where they did not keep to the rules they were expelled, for example *Medecins Sans Frontieres* (MSF) had to leave Ethiopia in 1985 when it protested against the government's forced repatriation scheme.

Since the end of the Cold War, relief has become increasingly involved with warfare, power and warlordism. This can include directly providing food, medicine or other supplies to one side in a conflict, by tolerating diversion of such materials, to providing an income by rental of premises, employment of staff, and purchasing and rental of equipment including vehicles. The cumulative effect of this may indeed prolong war situations. Strategic protection is also given by maintaining supplies to garrisons and relief shelters so that they do not become militarily vulnerable and keeping roads, airfields and ports open which would otherwise be closed.

More insidious, yet just as important, is the mere effect of a presence which provides legitimacy for a controlling authority. For example, NGO have to make contact with local and national political parties in order to function and this may seem like approval to those watching. Also, organisations which deliver humanitarian aid often espouse a concern for human rights, but if they remain silent witnesses to human rights abuses then to the outside world this can give the appearance that no such offences are being committed.

Since the Cold War the political climate in Africa has changed. Some African states no longer have a recognised government. Emergencies such as the Rwanda situation become long standing, and many relief agencies are obliged to work in them. One of the most important changes, however, is the reaction of western governments. With no strategic or commercial interests, their chief concern is to avoid bad publicity at home from humanitarian crises which have reached the media. Thus it can be seen that two counterbalancing effects have begun to occur – the developed world is disengaging itself from direct relief to poor countries, and in consequence there is an increase in donor-funded relief organisations. This has increased the political influence and power of all relief agencies. In addition to the primary responsibility of delivery of services, their traditional role, they now see part of their role as conflict resolution, human rights issues, together with the publicity, lobby and advocacy which goes with these functions. One extreme example of this was the call for international military intervention by NGOs in Somalia in 1992, in response to the undoubtedly severe human suffering caused by the unstable political situation. Operation Restore Hope resulted, but it had no accountability either to Somalia or the NGO working in Somalia, nor a full appreciation of the complex political context in which they were working. Similar calls by NGO for international military intervention were made in Rwanda to halt the advance of the RPF following the genocide. These calls were largely ignored but it could be argued that the advance of the RPF was more effective in halting the genocide than the UN could be. This is still open to debate. An Oxfam document (Vassall-Adams 1994) severely criticises the UN for lack of action, whereas African Rights considers that allowing the RPF to advance was the only possible solution at the time which could have resulted in the ending of the genocide (African Rights, November 1994).

Many relief organisations get most of their funding from governments in the developed world who are directing foreign aid towards non-governmental organisations, but for most aid agencies, a relatively small but important part of funding comes from individual donations. In order to continue with their humanitarian mission, organisations have to bow to the wishes of sponsors whose view is largely shaped by public opinion which in turn is influenced by the picture presented in the media. This means that aid is directed towards high profile emergencies. For example, following the Gulf War, few organisations were able to offer humanitarian aid in Iraq in spite of suffering of the innocent.

The United Nations role in relief organisations is to take responsibility for registering refugees via the United Nations High Commission for Refugees (UNHCR). The UNHCR also has a role in protecting human rights of refugees.

Whenever there is a humanitarian crisis and the media become involved, the horrific story is spread and the watching world states that something must be done. As aid agencies arrive, our televisions portray pictures of nurses laying hands on grateful sufferers and putting everything right. The press then find a new disaster and move on, leaving the impression that the crisis is now solved. This is a distorted view. Although emergencies inevitably do produce some medical needs, other demands such as providing food, clean water and latrines have a bigger life-saving impact. Inevitably local communities as well as the refugee population will have their share of skilled workers such as nurses, mechanics, engineers and drivers. The individual expatriate role is more managerial, administrative and organisational and is there to monitor the use of resources provided by donors.

My Call To Burundi

Compassionate and caring people often feel moved at the possibility of alleviating human suffering and imagine they would like to go to areas of desperate human need to offer their time and love. But there is *no* point in sending unskilled but highly concerned individuals to any project in the underdeveloped world. There are already enough mouths to fill and plenty of unskilled labour on hand. Relief agencies are very selective when choosing overseas staff. Potential employees need to demonstrate that they can offer specific skills and also the right personality to be able to cope and take a wide view of the situation which they will confront.

I am a nurse, and my only overseas experience had been a few weeks in Romania several years beforehand. This was an obvious disadvantage. My advantage was that I had considerable management qualifications and experience in health care settings. My particular skill is in setting up management systems. I respond to challenges and the possibility of working in overseas settings stretched my imagination and stimulated me in a way that no other job could.

I had first had the dream to work overseas as a teenager. After training as a nurse I married and had three wonderful children, and I saw my responsibility then as joining forces with my partner to ensure that my family had a secure and happy upbringing. As my family became older, my old ambition returned, until eventually the pull became irresistible, compelling and overpowering. But in many ways it was also selfish. I was leaving behind my family and doing something just for myself.

Before volunteering for overseas work, this had long been discussed with my family. They fully supported me because they understood how much I wanted to go. This was different to facing the reality of the situation when a post was offered to me. I was offered a six-month contract in Burundi working in a health project in a refugee camp. From then on, I was in a state of hectic preparation and excited anticipation which my husband, David, could not share. What he felt was a mixture of anger because I was leaving him, envious that I was going away to have an exciting adventure, worried because Burundi was an unstable country, redundant because he could not take the traditional male protective role when I was there. For every aid worker that goes overseas the families left have to be brave and courageous, whereas the workers themselves are irresistibly and sometimes unreasonably drawn towards their destiny.

I left my family and England on 25th February, one week later than originally planned because of an outburst of violence in Burundi, which had meant all expatriate staff had been evacuated to Rwanda for a few days until the trouble settled down. I arrived early on 26th February in Bujumbura, the capital of Burundi.

Bujumbura is on the shores of Lake Tanganyika in the Rift Valley which divides East and West Africa. It is hot and humid, and comparatively sophisticated when compared to many other towns in Africa. The town centre showed signs of lack of investment with pot-holed roads and boarded-up shops. It was Sunday when I arrived and it was not until Monday that I realised just how populated this country was when I saw dual carriageways full of people, walking four to ten abreast, and stretching as far as the eye could see, on their way to school and work.

On the outskirts of town, the roads were red dirt track and lined with bungalows and houses, all protected by high walls and tall gates, but not unattractive, as over these walls cascaded a wide variety of lush and attractive shrubs of all colours. It was in two of these houses that CONCERN were located, one in which staff stayed and one which housed the Burundian headquarters of CONCERN. There were two staff in Bujumbura, both French speaking – Rob, the country representative, and Anne, the administrator.

This was a gentle introduction to my life in Burundi. First of all, my briefings particularly related to security issues. In a country with poor communication systems and unstable politics, an important lesson is how to use the Codan radios which are located in the cars, houses and offices. There is a curfew both in Bujumbura and in Kirundo, which means that all people have to stay indoors from dusk at 7 p.m. until dawn.

The following day I was transported by land cruiser to Kirundo, which is in the north of Burundi, along a surprisingly good tarmac road. As we rose up from the Rift Valley to the mountainous plateau which covers most of Burundi, the weather became notably cooler and at times it felt too cool to be wearing only jeans and a tee-shirt. Burundi is beautiful, rustic and fertile, lush and green. Most of the scenery is serenely rural rather than spectacular, but from time to time a breathtaking view appears. One such view was about thirty minutes away from Bujumbura, where across the hills I could see the Rift Valley and Lake Tanganyika stretching apparently endlessly into the distance. The hills near Bujumbura are not rounded but form sharp peaks and deep valleys. Everywhere is cultivated, however steep the slope. The crops are varied in small plots and holdings. In amongst the fields are dotted a few small houses or hovels. They are mostly of stone or red mud bricks, some with windows and doors but many with just a hole for an entrance. The roofs are made of pan tiles, corrugated tin or occasionally thatch. Often they are shaded by banana palms or yellow flowered acacia. Along the road were shiny coated cattle with huge horns or sometimes a few goats or chickens. From time to time we passed through a small township with a few houses, a marketplace, perhaps a petrol station, and a shop.

And lots of people! They were everywhere. In the fields the women worked in their bright coloured sarongs and headscarves, babies on their back, and scythes in their hands as they tilled the fields. Men meanwhile seemed to sit in sullen groups or walked along the side of the road. There were not many vehicles, but lots of heavily laden bicycles, their riders clinging dangerously to the back of lorries, which gave them a tow up to the top of the incline. The graceful and attractive people all looked healthy, but as we got further away from the capital they seemed to be dirtier and more poorly dressed.

Along the road we passed through various checkpoints. These were manned by soldiers who carefully examined our documents before opening the piece of string carelessly strung across the road which acted as a barrier, and then they waved us on with their rifles. I understand that failure to stop can result in being shot or the driver being taken to prison.

At 2 p.m., four hours after leaving Bujumbura, I arrived at my new home and was dumped by the driver who sped off, leaving me alone in my new house. Communication had not been easy as he spoke no English, and I only spoke a few words of French. The house was a large basically equipped and furnished bungalow on the edge of the town of Kirundo. After a time, the team leader and health coordinator, an Irish nurse called Maddy, arrived. She showed me around. We had water in the tap, a cold water shower, electricity for two hours in the evening when the generator worked, and occasional use of a TV. I was to share this house with Pat, a Catholic nun. There were two other CONCERN bungalows within easy walking distance, which housed the rest of the expatriate team. This consisted of Maddy, Emer the administrator, Andre the doctor, Meduoc the logistics manager, and Mike the engineer. The houses were staffed by local Burundian staff who cleaned, attended to our laundry, and cooked an apparently monotonous variety of local foods.

Pat was a very down-to-earth person who was of Scottish descent. She had converted to Roman Catholicism during her early life and became a nun aged twenty-four. Although she was now nearly sixty, she was full of energy and had considerable experience of conflict situations, having worked in Angola, Mozambique, Zimbabwe, Zaire, and Tanzania, before arriving in Burundi. She straightaway took me under her wing and taught me a great deal, not only about security issues and work, but also about how to live in a house which had erratic utilities.

The expatriate teams had armed guards. Pat and I had two CONCERN unarmed guards at night, and two armed guards twenty-four hours a day, who were provided by the Burundi army. In time, this became oppressive. Apparently there had been very little trouble in Kirundo immediately prior to my arrival; trouble when it did occur was likely to be in the town itself, and we were a little way out of town. I never felt at risk in all of the time I lived in Burundi. I suppose it's like living in a rough inner city district or in the shadow of a nuclear power station. Outsiders perceive a danger, but when you are on the inside you feel that if you play by the rules you'll be all right. Pat had arrived a month or so before me and she had not heard any rifle fire or grenades. This sort of sound is commonplace in Bujumbura; I had heard distant grenades during my one night there. Another important security point was our two-way radios which we carried on our person at all times. These had a limited range of a few miles so we could not contact Kirundo when we were in the camp, but expatriate and Burundi managerial staff could contact each other in the camp, or after curfew we could talk to any of the team who lived in other houses if a need arose.

The main worry of mine before I arrived had been health issues. Before leaving England I had attended a briefing in Dublin. There, the health risks were stressed. Rob and Pat both seemed to consider malaria as the greatest risk, and Rob had just got over malaria the previous week, which emphasised the point. I had been warned about not drinking the local water. The water we drank was boiled and filtered before we used it. The water from the tap originated in the local lake. It was stored in a huge yellow bladder tank in the garden which looked like an oversize hot water bottle and was filled by water tanker. Pat assured me it was safe to use for cleaning teeth. We also had salad for tea which looked the most inviting part of the meal. I had been warned not to eat salad unless I checked that it had been washed with filtered water, but everyone else tucked in, so I did too. The disease risk seemed to be less of a problem than I had imagined it would be before I arrived.

So now I had found out where I was to live and with whom I was to share my life with for the next few months. I looked at all of my family photos before I went to bed and wished I'd got pictures of my friends too. My mind was scanning and thinking of them all. I set my alarm so that it would go off at dawn, 6 a.m..

Work At The Camp; First Impression

Pat was in charge of a department which she set up called Maternal and Child Health, or MCH. This was largely to do with preventative medicine. Before she arrived there was no immunisation programme or screening programme for children and no antenatal care. She had set up a programme which now seemed to be very organised. She had an interpreter called Faustin and I had an interpreter called Cyprien. My work was to be in the hospital eventually, but there was no one to hand over to me, as the previous nurse had left a few weeks before I arrived. Pat and I decided that it would be best if I worked with her in MCH for the first week in order to orientate to African medicines and procedures. The following week she was going on leave and I could take over her work, and then on her return I would move to the Curative Care Department, which I would run together with Andre, the doctor, and Tharcisse, a Burundian who was employed as the clinic and hospital manager. The departments for which I would be responsible consisted of a clinic, dressing room, day hospital, and dysentery unit.

There was a lot to learn. Pat was the only nurse at the time in MCH, although eventually she hoped to have a local qualified nurse to join her in her department. But until she arrived, Pat had to do all of the consultations. We sat at a desk, and women and children entered when we called "Undi" which I think meant "next". All of the children under two years of age were being registered with MCH and were being weighed and measured by refugees that Pat had trained. We then examined the children for signs of disease. Worms, anaemia and scabies were quite common. Tapeworms can make children really ill. We then tried to find out if they had immunisations in Rwanda and then started them on an immunisation programme. Their cards were marked accordingly, and they then entered the immunisation room where trained refugees administered the course of treatment as prescribed. The pregnant women also came to be checked to see if all was well; there were local traditional birth attendants, a technical assistant, and a midwife, who checked them and if there was a problem they had to be referred to Pat.

Part of our work was to decide who had extra food. Refugees get a basic food supply, but if they had extra need of food – for example, if they were pregnant or lactating – they got a supplementary addition, and if they were very seriously underweight they could be referred for therapeutic feeding, which was a very high-calorie ration. Cards were filled out for appropriate referrals, and as everyone seemed to try to get extra food this was an important component of the work of the expatriate staff, to decide who is genuine and who is not. One of the diseases of malnutrition is called Kwashikor and it is a protein deficiency which causes oedema. Podgy and overweight babies were bought to us sometimes and the mums tried to convince us that the layers of fat were oedema. Turning someone away inevitably meant that they were extremely cross with us and stood looking daggers at a distance at us in the hope that this would make us change our mind.

During the first day we saw about seventy babies and thirty to forty pregnant mothers. In between, a few problems arose which we had to deal with immediately. One was an orphan baby girl whose uncles and aunts refused to take her into their family to care for, and we had to immediately contact some Sisters who ran an orphanage to get her admitted. Another was a child with a bean in his ear. This is apparently quite an emergency, as the bean will quickly grow and perforate the drum if it is not removed. So he had to go by car to the hospital in Kirundo where they had facilities for removing it. We also had to attend a weekly camp meeting, which was conducted mainly in French. Local staff and refugees who managed different departments, such as sanitation, health education, hospital services and therapeutic feeding services, came to the meeting. Most of the meeting had to be translated. There were certain items on the agenda which seemed to be very repetitive and did not achieve much, for example, problems in digging latrines, and the whole meeting seemed to become long-winded and rather boring. Some things are the same all over the world! Our day finished at 4 p.m., although we still had about a hundred people waiting to see us, and we had to ask them to return the following day. We had to get back to Kirundo about half an hour's drive away before curfew.

When we got back, Pat went for a French lesson. I decided that while she was out I had better sort out a system for washing myself. In a house with no electricity before nightfall, only one small gas ring, no hot water, a dribbling cold water supply, an erratic, cold and wildly uncontrollable shower, a sink with a plug which does not fit, getting clean is all part of the day's challenge. When Pat returned, I was clean and she triumphantly produced a large bottle of beer which she had been given. We sat down to our meal, washed it down with the alcoholic gift, discussed ways of livening up the menu, and then the generator started up and we had electricity. This week we had the TV so we hastily stopped everything to put on a video. Halfway through the generator failed – we had to resort to reading and writing by excellent solar lamps. The following day we had a car returning from Kirundo to Bujumbura. This was our only way of getting post home so the lack of entertainment gave me a good opportunity to write lots of news to send home.

Being away from home and in an environment which was so totally different, with people I had never met before had a strange effect on my perception of the passing of time. By the second day I had a strange feeling that I had lived in Africa for months; home almost seemed a distant memory. My emotions were split between times of yearning for home and everyone there, and times of total absorption in this topsy-turvy place.

The next morning was wonderful – clear blue skies and sunshine as we made our way to work. We seemed to drive along a peninsular of land with views of lakes on both sides of the road. The road is a red dirt track, and on each side there is lush vegetation, and edging the road were hovels made out of sticks and mud mostly with corrugated roofs, but some covered with the traditional banana leaves. Each house was surrounded by a garden or farm, depending on your point of view. They grow bananas, coffee beans, sweet potatoes, cassava, french beans. The houses are shaded by acacia trees with their bright yellow flowers. The children rushed out to wave to us as we went past. The roads were full of people, walking mostly, but there were a few cyclists with crates of beer on the back so heavily laden that I wondered how they kept upright on the heavily pitted and uneven road. A lot of the walkers carried baskets with produce from their farm on their heads, on the way to a market somewhere to sell their surplus produce.

The land cruiser in which we travelled to work was driven by a young Burundian called Justin. Pat was convinced that he drove at breakneck speed, and at intervals of about two minutes she told him to drive more slowly, making noises of mock-terror to emphasise her point. In the back of the car we had a crowd of Kirundo people who worked in the camp, mostly nurses and administrators. Pat thought it was like being on a school bus, and I had to agree that it was noisy, although the chatter was a novelty for me and I didn't find it at all distressing. On the way we stopped at the local hospital for vaccine and the CONCERN office in Kirundo town to collect anything which we needed for the camp.

We travelled through three armed checkpoints. One was manned by a soldier, the boyfriend of a midwife who travelled in the land cruiser. We usually stopped so that they could have a brief chat before continuing. Just past the last checkpoint we could see the huge array of bright blue buildings which housed the school. The buildings were big enough for 5,000 pupils, but at that time they needed teachers and latrines before the school could be fully operational. The camp itself had a long name, Rukuramigabo, but everyone called it Ruku.

The camp consisted of thousands of huts, called *blunde*, made from blue plastic sheeting which was provided by the United Nations. They were about the size of a small garden shed, and each one housed a family of up to eight persons. When they arrived, each family was given a plastic sheet and it was up to them how they built their shelter. Some camps apparently have enterprising refugees who grow vegetables around their *blunde*, but so far ours hadn't done so, although the ground was fertile enough. Africans are an enterprising lot. A huge market had grown at the entrance to the camp. You could buy anything there, from perfectly tailored trousers to doughnuts, from mats made of rushes to all types of cereal and vegetables. There was even a licensed restaurant! The market would make many traders at home feel envious as it was usually full of people. The best buy was avocados, priced at three for twenty Burundian Francs (BF). They were huge and beautiful. At an exchange rate of 250 BF to the American dollar, this made them a bargain.

The refugees were in the main well-fed, some even plump, and most were well-clothed, although some were dirty and a few had clothes which had fallen into holes. At the time I arrived they were provided with 1,900 Kcal per day per refugee. This was decreasing to 1,500 Kcal the following week, and after that it was rumoured that it would fall to 800 Kcal. This was because donor countries were getting less generous with Rwandans, and the feeling was that reducing rations could encourage refugees to return to their homeland. This normally fertile land had a bumper crop this year and although the crop had been low in Rwanda, it was because of the lack of manpower which had left land untitled and crops unpicked. On the other hand, the fear of finding someone else settled and farming on your land from the opposing tribe can be a real disincentive to returning home, when the ethnic fear is so great and there is no legal system to uphold your claim.

The second night in Kirundo we had a rainstorm, and yes, it caused the generator to give up again! But we managed to finish watching the second half of the video before we were plunged into darkness.

The days were falling into a routine.

6.30 a.m. – My alarm went off. I discovered that 6.30 a.m. exists! I did my exercises, had a quick wash while waiting for the kettle to boil. Breakfast consisted of banana, local bread which was very pleasant when fresh, local cheese when I could get it, and tea. I got used to drinking tea black because of the shortage of milk. I ate breakfast while I listened to the BBC World News, although the reception was not always good.

7.15 a.m. – The driver arrived and we were off to camp. The drive was about five miles.

8 a.m. – We arrived at the camp and began work.

12.30 p.m. – We had lunch, sometimes walking around the market and sometimes sitting in Pat's office. We sometimes had an avocado for lunch or at other times I had tomato and bread.

1.30 p.m. – Work again.

4 p.m. – Journey home.

5 p.m. – Arrived in Kirundo and did any work in the office there as necessary.

5–7 p.m. – We usually had meetings at this time.

7 p.m. – Curfew time: we prepared and ate supper. Initially dinner was cooked by our cook, Michel, but eventually we cooked most of our food ourselves. We gave up eating meat which was usually tough and not very appetising, although sometimes goat was edible and tender. Instead we ate fish from the local lake, omelette, and sometimes we found a tin of meat or salmon in our store cupboard. This we ate with potatoes, rice and vegetables. The vegetables were cabbage, tomato, avocado, onion, and haricot beans. Occasionally we managed to get some carrots, turnips and cauliflower.

7.30–10 p.m. – Locked in due to curfew, watching TV when we had electricity, reading, or writing by the light of solar lamps, or doing crosswords or playing scrabble.

10 p.m. – Wash and bed, and depending on how long the solar lights lasted I wrote letters and read.

While driving to work I had chance to look at Kirundo. It was a small town and the capital of a province of the same name. It consisted of the usual ramshackle collection of African houses, made of concrete, generally in bad repair with rusty bits of concrete and railings. All around there were deep ditches, some several feet deep, and after seeing the rain here I understood why. It had a marketplace which was open two days a week including Sunday. The market had covered stalls as well as space for traders to put their mats and produce on display on the floor. The main thing to say about Kirundo was that it was at the end of the tarmac road which linked it to Bujumbura, but the road was being extended through the town and it was full of diggers, lorries, stones, workmen, and piles of sand. Vehicles had to negotiate through a maze of uncontrolled road-making equipment making life extremely hazardous – a motorcyclist was killed during the week after a road accident.

Kirundo had a hospital not far from the houses in which CONCERN staff lived. It too was undergoing major changes, as new ditches were being dug in the grounds. There were also a few shops in the centre of the town, particularly shops which sold material. Outside each shop sat a tailor or seamstress, who would sew anything you ordered. Inside they were full of wonderful material in bright yellows, oranges, reds, and greens. There was a mosque in town; I saw a few Muslims who could be recognised by their distinctive clothing. There was apparently a Pentecostal church in a nearby settlement, but the main church was a Catholic church, the size of a cathedral, a mile or so out of town, and situated at the most amazing location – overlooking a wide and awesome view of the hills of Burundi. There was also a convent there, the orphanage, and a centre for handicapped children. Apparently it was a Tutsi town, although personally I was not able to tell the difference between the two groups. People say Tutsi are taller with a narrower nose and higher forehead, but they are so intermarried that I found it was difficult to identify ethnic origins easily.

During the first week Rob, the country representative, had arrived from Bujumbura to attend a meeting with the Governor of Kirundo. The governor had to be a brave chap as his two predecessors had been assassinated. The meeting was, as usual, connected to security issues. Apparently MSF are considering pulling out of Burundi due to security problems. Rob was assured that although the French were not well-liked, which put MSF at risk, CONCERN were well thought of, and the local community would continue to give us full support. Apparently, the French were involved in Rwandan politics and it was thought by some people that they had favoured the previous government in Rwanda and had supplied them with arms. There was certainly no evidence of problems in Kirundo, which remained very quiet, but when we listened to the African News Service at 7 p.m., we heard there had been a skirmish between troops and Hutus on the Burundi border although no one had been hurt.

By the Friday of my first week I was starting to get to know everyone and find my way round. My interpreter, Cyprien, was about twenty-one but looked sixteen. He spoke French, English, and the local dialect. He was studying at college and planned to go to university when war broke out. He would never return there. Another really intelligent boy called Vincent worked in MCH and he was taking a biology degree when the war broke out. Yet, for them there was no future, and those people were the real victims of the Rwandan War.

I was starting to look around my department. It included a dressing room with two dressing technicians. The room was filthy; mud on the walls, the sink, the chairs, as well as forming a thick coat on the floor. One wound oozed blood all over the dressing stool, which was then washed with about two tablespoons of water. It was transferred to a pool of mud on the floor, and into it stepped the barefooted refugees. This in a continent where estimation of HIV infections is usually considered to be about 20%. The floor was rough concrete and it was not possible to wash it. I saw Mike, the engineer, to see if he could do anything to make it easier to clean. Despite all of this filth, I was amazed to see some really well-healed wounds. One was a child who had burned the whole forearm except for his fingers, and despite the horrors of the treatment room, it appeared to be healing well.

I took photographs around the camp for people at home. There was a tent for newly-delivered mothers where I took three snapshots. Later on, the mothers held up their babies for me to take a photo every time I walked past. Mothers there had lots of children, and Pat, despite her Catholic faith, was determined to put an end to that and was starting up a birth control clinic. Babies were fed in a traditional way, mothers walk round with breasts on show, and if the baby is hungry, he or she grabs one! Of course, they are mostly carried on the back. The mother bends forward and the baby is placed on her back in one deft movement. Even small babies seem to know they have to grab and hang on, legs astride mum's back. They are then tied on with a wide piece of usually knitted cloth which is tied at the front, top first. The lower portions of the cloth were pulled tight under junior's buttocks, and then the lower corners were tied at the front. The whole baby and holder was then covered by a piece of brightly coloured sarong which the mother wore. No nappies and no nappy rashes. Surprisingly, neither mother or baby seemed to smell of urine at all, although there was often a very acidic body odour smell. After one week, I discovered a very interesting question. In the first week I had examined hundreds of babies and not one of them was soiled. Where do African babies poop?

The fathers sometimes appeared at the clinic, but would hold their babies in their arms just as Europeans would. Every time Pat saw a man in the clinic he was dragged off to her family planning room. If they asked for more food, Pat gave a set answer – with fewer babies there would be more food to go round. And yet there was a perverse incentive for people to have babies: pregnant and lactating women have larger rations. When a new baby arrives, rations are increased for that family.

One of the difficulties in starting work in my unit was the problem of finding out what my predecessor had done. But I could see that there was a problem of overspending, lack of control, poor practice, unsupervised work, waste, and petty pilfering. Writing a set of rules in the form of a simple quality manual would help not only the work but it would be a guide to any persons who followed me. This I decided would be my goal at Ruku camp.

I also made a decision about contacting people at home. There was a horrendously expensive satellite fax in Kirundo. I decided that once a week I would use it and ask them to fax me as well, as I was desperate for news of home.

Settling Down

Having sent a fax to David with details of how to contact me, later the same day, just one week after arriving in Burundi, I received a fax from home. I can't describe what it meant. Suddenly I felt part of my family again, instead of feeling a sense of alienation. I heard that my son had been accepted for a nurse training course and that my family, and especially David, were missing me as I knew they would be. I read the one page fax over and over again, not only that day but for days and weeks afterwards. Having a communication from home is in many ways unsettling and tear provoking, but is a necessary part of coming to terms with your new existence.

In this part of Africa white faces were not usual. In Kirundo province, five of our team were white, there were three white French MSF workers who ran a clinic service for local Burundians, a Russian surgeon who worked in the hospital, three Italian Sisters who lived at the convent and operated social services at the camp, one Frenchman who ran an EC engineering project, and one Greek who worked for the Catholic Relief Services, who provided food for Burundian displaced persons. Everywhere I went I was seen as different, and the lack of privacy and feeling of being on show was in some ways amusing and in other ways limiting and oppressive.

Firstly there was the constant pressure of having armed guards. They slept in a tent inside the garden of the house. They did not try to be intrusive but they were there. One thing which I found very irritating was a card game which they constantly played, which meant that they had to slap cards down on a hard surface. The regular slapping noise on an otherwise quiet Sunday afternoon seemed to intrude into my personal space, and somehow, no matter where I was in the house or garden, I could hear it. Other people found different things about the guards annoyed them – for example, they frequently drank heavily and begged for beer when they had run out of their own supplies, they talked at night sometimes, they had local women visit them in their tent, they sat in a position where they could stare inside the house and watch what you were doing. What one person tolerates as acceptable, another person will find totally constricting and irritating!

Everywhere I went people watched me. If I walked in the market people would shout to me or follow me, children would rush up and try to hold my hand. When I was driven to work in the land cruiser, children, and occasionally adults, would rush out of their houses to wave to me. Sometimes they would put out their hands, palm uppermost, in a begging fashion. This I found distressing because it seemed to demonstrate a willingness for Africans to put themselves into a position of inferiority and thus demean themselves. I would rather I had met a proud and disdainful attitude which would at least have demonstrated a sense of self-worth. Perhaps Africans do not value privacy in the way that we Europeans do. In any case, they felt it was acceptable to peer at white people at any time, looking through holes in the fence of the garden, trying to sell flowers and vegetables over the tall garden fence. This together with the presence of the guards made sitting in the garden an ordeal rather than a pleasure.

One day I attempted a quiet walk in the countryside near Kirundo. It was impossible. In the distance were two boys carrying bundles of wood on their head. As soon as they saw me they dropped their firewood in the field and galloped at pace across the field to meet me. They were soon joined by two more who carried jerrycans full of water on their heads, then two more, until in the end I had about twenty children following me and chattering away in French, feeling very amused at my poor command of the language. I felt a bit like the Pied Piper. I caught the word "*voiture*" and realised that they were asking why I was not in a car. I replied "*J'aime marcher*", which seemed to cause them considerable amusement, or at least, it caused most of them to lie on the floor shaking their arms and legs in the air with a look of joy on their faces. I enjoyed the occasion, but I knew that it would get wearing if at any time you needed solitude, as this was impossible to obtain.

Another difficulty I encountered was the change to living in an enclosed environment with one other person when I had previously lived in a house as one of six adults, all of whom had plenty to do and plenty of friends. When I was at home, most evenings we went our own way and did our own thing, meeting up for a talk, a meal, or a trip to the pub as we wanted. There were times in the evening when everyone was busy and occupied and no one knew where I was or what I was doing; this gave me some space for myself.

When I moved to Kirundo, Pat was extremely kind to me and tried to make me feel at home. We were cooped up together, seven evenings a week, as well as working together. Pat, out of thoughtfulness, always took an interest in everything I was doing every evening, but sometimes this felt overpowering as it took away my final privacy. It was difficult to talk to her about it, because she was trying her utmost to make up for me being away from my family and friends and missing them. I could never find the right words or moment to explain to her that what I missed most of all was the opportunity to control any aspect of my own life and the need not to be noticed sometimes. This was part of the stress of working overseas.

This was the downside. The upside was that I had a challenging and stimulating job surrounded by fascinating people and meeting new problems which were not easy to solve. In spite of all of the homesickness, frustration, and constrictions to my life, I felt happier and more fulfilled than perhaps ever before. To me this was the best job in the world, and every day I wanted to be part of the team in Kirundo more than anything else.

I said earlier that our role was one of establishing control systems. The therapeutic feeding centre was managed by a refugee called Charles, who was an educated man and who spoke excellent English. One of the difficulties faced by a refugee in this situation is that food is a precious commodity, really it is the *currency* of the refugee camp. Refugees are not necessarily sweet-natured and grateful; this population came from a violent and corrupt country. If Charles was asked to give a refugee food and refused, then in some cases he and his family would be at risk. In consequence, many people were admitted to the unit for extra food when they had no particular nutritional need, but enough power to persuade the management that they should be entered on the feeding programme. This was one of the problems which we set out to tackle. The first thing was to take the responsibility for admission and discharge away from Charles; this was something he welcomed.

The expatriate team agreed on a criteria for referral to the therapeutic feeding, and Charles agreed that he would not admit anyone without our authority. We also agreed on a review date on which all cases would be seen and discharged if they no longer met the criteria. The criteria was based either on previous medical history – for example, someone who had just had a severe bout of measles or dysentery might be admitted for a two-week stay, or because they were seriously underweight. In this camp, which had been established for a year, less than 1% were seriously malnourished. I did see one case of Kwashikor, which is a protein deficiency disease where children have the characteristic pot bellies and moon faces caused by oedema, and two cases where children were generally severely underweight and undernourished. It is possible that these few children suffered from Aids, which might have been the cause of their weight loss rather than malnutrition.

My department was Curative Care. The buildings were made of bamboo and black plastic sheeting, with very high windows under the eaves and open doorways. Refugees who felt ill came to the clinic. This consisted of a large waiting area, five consulting rooms, and a dressing room. In each consulting room there was a doctor or a nurse and a dispenser of drugs. The drugs which were available were limited; in the main they consisted of antibiotics, vitamins, analgesics, drugs for indigestion and anti-malarial.

Any patient who could be cared for by their relatives were sent back to their *blunde*. If they were very ill, and particularly if they had a temperature of over 40°, they were admitted to the hospital. This was a day hospital; it had to close at night for security reasons. But in this hospital patients could have infusions, injections, and cold compresses for fever. The care was still carried out by a *'guarde malade'*, a family member who stayed with the person who was ill. The specific medical and nursing tasks were carried out by two auxiliary nurses. If there was an epidemic, such as measles, then a tent would be put up outside the main day hospital so that it would be possible to isolate people with infectious diseases from others.

The dysentery unit treated everyone with diarrhoea, having its own clinic, day hospital, and latrines. Dysentery tends to be a big problem when camps are first established, before latrines are dug and clean water supplies organised, but following this acute stage, the number of sufferers fall dramatically.

The pharmacy was also under my responsibility. As it needed to be secure, it was located in part of the MCH building which was built of brick. The main pharmacy stores were in Kirundo, but the Ruku pharmacy should have kept enough supplies for a week or so in the camp. Because drugs commanded a high price in the market, particularly antibiotics which could be used for venereal diseases, they had to be very carefully recorded to ensure that the possibility of pilfering was reduced.

There were no registration systems for healthcare, no way of recording past medical histories or drugs given, no treatment protocols, no job descriptions, no staff training systems, no work supervision except in an *ad hoc* fashion or under the most vague terms, no audits, no inventories, no ordering systems. Two departments, which were the Supplementary Feeding and Health Education, had no supervision at all. The therapeutic feeding unit had only just come under the control of the expatriate team. This was not a criticism but an acknowledgement of the stage we had reached in this camp. Up until this point, the work had been to set up services, and it had to keep pace with demand as the emergency unfolded and 27,000 people moved to Ruku camp. Initially it was assumed that when the political situation changed, the refugees would return, but this had not happened. Because the crisis was over, it was time to install mechanisms to ensure that money was spent effectively and that resources were not wasted by poor or corrupt practice. This was the reason why I found the job so attractive. Setting up control mechanisms and management systems was my area of expertise. As I gradually came to grips with the lack of organisation which existed, the possibilities for me to put my own stamp on things and making them more efficient and effective caused me to feel excited at the challenge ahead of me.

One of the ways in which the camp was being made more efficient was an improvement in food distribution systems. This was the responsibility of the International Red Cross in our camp and not part of CONCERN's work. The food which was distributed was maize, beans and oil, together with firewood, which was the only fuel available for cooking. The camp was divided into zones. Each zone had a Chef de Zone, and until the beginning of March the chef collected the ration and divided it amongst refugees living in his zone. This meant that the family and friends of the chef were more likely to get a generous ration, and anyone who displeased the chef might not get anything at all. Part of the ration could be creamed off and sold in the market.

The ration distribution was being altered at this point in time so that food was distributed to each family. Each family had a card which showed how many persons belonged to each family. The head of the household collected the allocated ration for his family every two weeks. This way there was less possibility of diversion or unfair allocation of food.

The first part of finding out what needed to be done was talking to staff and watching what happened. Fortunately, in this I found Tharcisse, the clinic manager, to be an excellent ally. Tharcisse had previously been an English teacher in Bujumbura, and so communicating with him was easy. He was also fair, well-liked, and a real extrovert. I also found that Tharcisse had a particular skill in dreaming up simple and effective little schemes in response to problems, so I learned to take problems which I had unearthed to him to work on. I also had to sit and watch dressings being done, patients being examined, drugs being dispensed, organisation of refugees in the waiting area, the cleaners cleaning, the hospital workers organising their work. There was a real difficulty here for me – I didn't know what was usual for Africa, what standard would be reasonable to impose, nor even what was the normal range of illnesses and treatments, and there was no real way of finding out, although Maddy and Pat were resources I could refer to when I had a particular problem. We also had a few textbooks to which I constantly referred.

The doctor in the clinic was Andre, an expatriate from Togo, who spoke excellent French but not very much English. As he was a real expert on African medicine, I could take advantage of his expertise in finding appropriate treatment of disease using the limited resources we had at our disposal. With the help of Cyprien, over a few weeks we discussed every common disorder which was likely to present in clinic and wrote out an examination, diagnosis, and treatment protocol for each.

Although this did not make me an expert on African medicine, I was no longer a complete novice. The common diseases which appeared in clinic were colds and chest infections, pyrexia which might have been due to malaria (we had no diagnostic aids), skin infections, gastritis (which was a particular problem as Rwandanese didn't usually eat maize in their diet at home and it was often not prepared properly), scabies, worms, simple diarrhoea, anaemia, ear and eye infections, general joint pains, and from time to time outbreaks of infectious illnesses. We had just had a measles outbreak. Every week there were a few people with broken bones, venereal disease, Aids, and tuberculosis.

When the patients arrived at the clinic, they were given a piece of paper on which their name was written and their temperature and weight recorded. When their turn came to enter the consultation room, this piece of paper was taken to the nurse. The nurse sometimes only examined the piece of paper before writing a prescription on it. At best they only seemed to ask a few basic questions before writing down a course of antibiotics which might or might not have been appropriate.

It didn't take long for me to become aware that people were being given costly drugs when they were simply not necessary. For example, there were cases which looked like simple colds which were treated with antibiotics, when I felt certain that in England the main treatment would be professional advice. But, as in England, it was often easier to see what was wrong and more difficult to think of a way of putting it right, especially when it meant changing the attitudes and work practices of all of the staff.

Initially when anyone starts a new job they feel totally lost, and for me, having worked with elderly people in England, the transition to working in a refugee camp, where most of the population was young adults and children, meant that the adjustment was huge. There were many times when I felt uncertain and insecure, times when I felt that my knowledge was non-existent, but there were never any times when I regretted being where I was. The difficulty for me was still coming to terms with the guilt I felt at leaving my family at home. Part of me thought that I had always had this dream, and had given my family twenty-four years of my life before I did a job which I had wanted to do more than anything else, and therefore I had done my bit. But a part of me also had to acknowledge that middle-aged mothers and wives usually stayed at home with their families, and by doing something for me I had put them all under great strain. David had got into the habit of calling me on the satellite phone from time to time – which cost about £6 *for each minute*. Additionally, because of our erratic electricity supply, it wasn't always easy for him to get through, and because of my work commitments and the curfew it was difficult for him to find a time when he could talk to me. The poor communications added to his frustration with a situation which he found difficult. David was very lonely at home, and I could understand that I had previously been part of every moment of his life. As well as being happily married to each other and sharing family and social commitments, we were also business partners and shared our working life too. When I left England, he had a big gap to fill and it wasn't easy. When he telephoned me, the first thing he had to do was tell me how unhappy he was; that was because I would normally be the person he would confide in. And by the time he had finished that, a quarter of an hour had passed and it was time to ring off. The telephone calls undoubtedly made us both feel worse.

Two weeks after my arrival, one Saturday I received two letters from home. They were to be the last letters I received for several weeks. One was from David writing down the events of his first week without me. From it I could see how miserable and unhappy he was. The second was from my son Alastair, who told me his news and how much he missed me. This was followed by one of David's phone calls. I went back to my room, lay on my bed, and howled in anguish. This was my worst moment. If you are with friends that you know quite well, you can feel justified in pouring your heart out to them. When you are with people you have only just met, you can't confide fully. They would soon get fed up with someone who constantly said, "I'm worried about my family". I did say it at times, and probably to the extent that it bored them. There were certainly no other mothers, nor anyone with a loving partner left at home, so they couldn't fully understand, but they had their own personal worries and individual pressures. My grief had to be coped with alone.

Security Problems

In general, since I had arrived in Kirundo, the security situation in Burundi, in particular in Bujumbura, had gradually become more tense. Things were relatively quiet in Kirundo. The exception to this was one night when a hand grenade went off quite close to the house. Pat was away and I was on my own, when I was awoken by a huge bang. I instantly knew what it was. For me it was a personal test and I could find out how I would react in a real life emergency situation. I could hear the guards running about outside, so I assumed that they would take any precautions necessary. I checked that my radio was switched on in case anyone needed to talk to me from one of the other houses, turned over, and went off to sleep again. In the morning we found out that the grenade had landed in the garden of the EC project coordinator, but it was intended for his neighbour's house where a local government official was staying. Whoever it was for, or whoever was guilty of throwing it, fortunately it hit a tree, was deflected, and did no damage. It might be that my reaction appeared too casual, and perhaps it was, but I had never felt myself to be a target of aggression and I assumed this incident to be yet another ethnic clash which was not likely to affect me.

Expatriates in Burundi had not really been targets of violent incidents. The exception to this was an European UN official who had been killed in Kirundo the previous year. Investigations of crime, including murder, were not easy in a country with limited policing and legal systems, and the motivation for any act of violence tended to be linked to rumour. Some people told me that the man who was killed was unlucky enough to be in the wrong place at the wrong time, and others thought that he had been selected for assassination by Hutu extremists because he had refused to allow arms to be taken into Ruku camp. CONCERN staff witnessed the killing, and it was said that the CONCERN nurse who tended him as he lay dying was put at risk herself. But this killing of an expatriate was not usual, as in Burundi, assassinations and murders were of Hutu and Tutsi almost without exception. It was thought that the population would not want to put at risk the overseas aid upon which the economy depended, by attacking aid workers.

During the beginning of March there had been increasing clashes between Hutu and Tutsi in Bujumbura. On 11th March Ernest Kabushemeye, the Energy and Mines Minister, was murdered. He was a member of the Hutu tribe, he belonged to a political party called Uprona, which was predominantly a Tutsi party, and he had resisted pressure which had been trying to persuade him to resign from Uprona. He was shot in the head outside a shop. In addition to this assassination, sporadic gunfire and grenade explosions had become more frequent early in March, and it was reported that twenty-nine Hutu had been killed in the capital. Tutsi youth were gathering in gangs at street corners and were setting up road blocks (Kiley, *Times*, 13.3.95).

The funeral of the minister was postponed when a mutilated and crucified body of a Tutsi government advisor, Lucien Sakub, was discovered on the 15th March. This was thought to be in retaliation for the murder of Kabushemeye (McGreal *Guardian* 17.3.95).

The ethnic distrust was present throughout the government, and a United Nations special mission to Burundi accused Uprona of systemic and persistent efforts to undermine the government. The human rights group Iteka also accused Uprona of calling a national strike and using armed gangs to enforce it. An Iteka spokesman stated that if you were using guns and grenades rather than the legitimate channels to force people into obeying your orders, then it could be assumed that people did not share your opinions. It was little wonder that news reports on television in England at that time were describing Burundi as a powder keg.

St Patrick's Day

Although Kirundo had in the past had a history of instability, it remained peaceful throughout this period. We were concerned in case there was a rise in tension in the camp as the ration had been cut. Hungry people get restless and aggressive. We had an expatriate team meeting once a week after work every Thursday, and inevitably, security was the item most commonly brought up on the agenda. It had been suggested that if things got difficult at the camp, then we would have to stay away until things settled down.

One of the other issues which was discussed, CONCERN being an Irish Organisation, was the St Patrick's day celebrations. Rob was away in Brussels on leave, and Anne was on her own in Bujumbura, and she had fixed up a party with a few other NGO at the CONCERN house. Emer, Andre, and I decided that we would go to join them. I did feel a little worried, as the unrest in Bujumbura was quite widely publicised on the BBC World News, but after Anne told us that it was relatively quiet in the suburb where the CONCERN house was situated, we decided to go.

We left on Friday 17th March on a beautiful clear and sunny morning and saw Burundi at its best. The road does not wind along the valleys but near the top of the hills, and it meant that we had sweeping views of the little farms stretching across the landscape with their well-tended little square fields, now all growing quickly as this time of the year was the rainy season.

On the way we stopped for lunch and we also called into an artisan centre. Emer was keen to learn to use the guitar and she wanted to see if she could get one made. The local craftsmen made beautifully finished wooden items - everything from carvings to ornaments, from furniture to musical instruments. After our leisurely journey we were due to arrive in Bujumbura at about 4.30 p.m.. About an hour before this, we had a call from Anne on our radio. We pulled in to the side of the road to take the call. We could see a few women in colourful costumes working in the fields. The sunshine was warm and the skies blue, and hardly a sound could be heard anywhere to interrupt our enjoyment in watching the scene in front of us. Anne rang to tell us to avoid the centre of Bujumbura as there was trouble there because of the funerals which were taking place that day of the two murdered government officials. It seemed totally incongruous to listen to the information we were receiving and contrast this with the apparent rural serenity of which we seemed to be a part at that moment. We skirted around the outskirts of Bujumbura and arrived at the CONCERN house without incident.

There were nine of us altogether for the St Patrick's party, from CONCERN, Oxfam, Red Cross, and Christian Aid. There were four Irish, three English, one French-Canadian, and one from Togo. The language spoken was a mixture of French and English. Everyone had to arrive before 7 p.m. and stay until the next morning. But it was really good to have a social function, as life with a curfew is so restricting. We had a meal cooked by Anne, washed down by beer and Irish-style coffee made with Scotch whisky! We danced a bit and chatted a lot and found out about the other people – for example, Bill from Christian Aid was meeting Amnesty International representatives the following morning to investigate claims of violation of human rights. It felt good to melt into the crowd, not to stand out as being different, and not to feel that I was being watched every moment.

The night was not too troubled. The gunfire and grenade noises were distant and not frequent, and the following morning it seemed that everything had settled down after the events of the day before, so Emer and I went to do some shopping. We bought two small mirrors for about £20. Things which are luxury items for Burundians are remarkably expensive. We then decided to set off for a beach about an hour's drive away from Bujumbura, where a hotel is situated on the edge of the lake.

It was perfect sunbathing weather. We swam in the lake and quite a long way further out we could see a hippo enjoying the coolness of the lake as well. On the way to the hotel we passed a sign on the edge of the road which announced that this had been the spot where Stanley met Livingstone. We lay on the beach until we got tanned by the sun, and then ate lunch in the hotel surrounded by monkeys who were hopeful that they would be able to steal our leftovers.

On Saturday evening, while everyone else went out, I had a long telephone call home. This was much more successful than the short and expensive satellite communications that we had previously endured. I spoke to David and all of my family for a long time, and at the end of it I felt much happier. David had decided to visit me in Burundi and he was planning to fly out in two weeks, so he felt much more relaxed and positive.

After a relaxing day, on Sunday we had a enjoyable return journey to Kirundo. We filled the car up with petrol, and as we waited in the queue, the petrol dispenser sprang a leak and the attendant had a petrol shower. It was amusing to see him leaping about to try to avoid getting a dousing. We passed a river, which was the local car wash, and cars were lined along the edge, their proud drivers washing off the mud to prepare the cars for their next week's work. We stopped to buy fruit and flowers at a stall in a village on the way home. Men were rushing about with baskets full of vegetables and huge bouquets of flowers, and if the item held aloft didn't seem to impress they scurried back to their spot on the pavement to swap it for another in the hope that we would find the new one more attractive. We eventually selected large bouquets for each of the three houses and two baskets of fresh vegetables. We used our local driver, Janvier, to do the negotiating, because we knew that he would get a better deal than we could. We arrived home in mid-afternoon. I felt relaxed and thought that the change had done me good. Our journey home was peaceful but it was not the same for everyone that evening.

Growing Troubles

To get back to Kirundo, we travelled north, out of Bujumbura. On the same evening on a road to the south of Bujumbura, three Belgians were killed together with the two Tutsi who accompanied them in the car. Other occupants of the car were injured and left for dead. The Belgians were apparently linked to the Red Cross. This was a definite assassination rather than a family caught up in crossfire. The tyres of their vehicle were shot out as it drove along the road, and then the occupants were all shot at point-blank range. Hutu extremists were suspected of the killing. Although in *The Guardian* on 21st March the targets were described as Tutsi, but when Anne went to a security meeting in Bujumbura, she was informed that the gun was directly aimed at the victims, and all indications were that they were purposefully shot. One of the victims was a child. This was a new turn of events for expatriate staff in Burundi, as it had been felt previously that foreigners were not considered to be part of the problem nor part of the solution, and therefore there was no point in killing them and causing outside countries to look unfavourably on Burundi.

As the situation became more tense, the communication network became very important and everyone seemed to want to glean any information they could get. Emer and Andre spoke fluent French and therefore they were able to listen to French and some local Burundian programmes on the radio. In our house we had two short wave radios and we listened extensively to the BBC World Service and Radio Africa which was on every evening. Whenever we met anyone from outside our town, we straightaway asked them if they had any information. If they had, this was immediately passed around our group by our portable radios. It was also useful for getting information from home, as this gave us an outside view on the situation. David became extremely anxious and he tried to ring me up several times each week. For me, I still did not feel worried about my own situation. This was not bravado, but I did not feel under threat. However, I was constantly worried about people at home, both friends and family, whom I knew were following the news of Burundi. This was now being widely reported on the television, and naturally my welfare was constantly on their mind. A further cause of worry was reports of the deaths of twenty-two people in a prison in Kigali. Seventy-five people were detained for questioning concerning the massacres of the previous year, and they were put into a cell designed for ten. In consequence, a number of the detained persons suffocated.

Of course, the main supply of information about the deteriorating situation in Bujumbura came from Anne who was on her own in the CONCERN house. Although she always sounded calm on the radio, we all were worried about her and we knew that she was under considerable stress. Her situation was one which we all disliked and she was never far from our thoughts, although we all felt unable to offer anything but our verbal support over the radio. The roads out of Bujumbura were not safe, as the gunfire and grenade attacks were now not limited to night time, only but occurred at any time. The market in Bujumbura was closed because of the violence and most of the town centre was closed. Anne took the decision that it was safer to stay where she was at the time than to try to move. One of the particular problems when there is ethnic unrest is that drivers will not escort expatriates out of the area of conflict. If they do so, their action may be construed as desertion by their own tribe and they and their families could be at risk. By the 21st March, *The Guardian* reported: "Burundi's demographic time bomb ticks louder than ever". The article proceeded to describe a "balance of terror" where the Hutu had the numbers, and the Tutsi had control of the army and considerable political power. It outlined the problems of the Tutsi hard-liners, who had consistently refused to develop a judiciary in Burundi, so that the Hutu would feel they had resource to legal protection, which could end the impunity with which Tutsi soldiers and extremists persecuted Hutus.

The Independent newspaper the following day reported: "Burundi on brink of an orgy of killing". One district, Bwiza, which was ethnically mixed, was a particular source of conflict. This was not far from the CONCERN house. Anne was on her own with two unarmed guards. The guards had to hide in the garage because of the stray bullets which were entering the garden. One of the CONCERN mechanics, John, was temporarily staying in Kirundo, where he was trying to fix up a more reliable generator for us. He decided to go to Bujumbura with his Ugandan driver, Moussa, to try to buy spare parts, which he needed for his repair work, but also to give Anne support and to consider the possibility of her evacuation to Kirundo. We were all relieved when we heard that he had arrived safely at the CONCERN house. He travelled to Bujumbura on Wednesday when the reports were of a heavier army presence, and in consequence fewer people were being killed.

Life At The Camp

During all of this time, work was continuing as normal for us. Pat had returned from leave. She had stayed in Kenya and had an suffered an accident there, sustaining fractures to two ribs, but she had insisted in returning to work. The refugees were obviously feeling very tense. On Tuesday, a loud bang was heard when a lorry backed into the water tank. People waiting in the clinic area started to scream loudly and ran away from the noise along a corridor. I was in the dressing room, just off the corridor and we quickly shut the door. My own reaction was one of total alertness and anxiety for a few moments until the screaming subsided and it became obvious that it was a false alarm. But you can hardly blame these people for feeling so tense when they had been witness to massacres on such a large scale less than a year before.

But, for the most part, the work was very routine. I had seen some interesting cases. For example, a child of about three or four years with 10% burns, had her wounds dressed in the dressing room. She was given lots to drink and then walked back to her *blunde* with her mother. I saw a young baby of one month with whooping cough and a case of extremely severe anaemia following malaria. The malarial parasite lives in red blood cells, and the blood cells are destroyed as the disease progresses.

I had started to look at quality systems and control mechanisms, and part of my work for this was to go through records of drug prescription in the clinic to see if the amount of drugs prescribed and dispensed to refugees was approximately the same as the amount of drugs which were requested from pharmacy. If there were large discrepancies, then this would point to stealing or corruption. One of the problems of the week was that we were running very low on many drugs, and in particular many antibiotics were completely gone. We ordered drugs from Dublin, and a large order arrived in Kirundo every three months and this was due soon. It is difficult to persuade the nurses not to prescribe antibiotics for every person who attends clinic, and over-prescribing was one of the reasons why we had run out of some medication. Although this did cause frustration and almost inevitably some deaths, it did bring home to the nurses that there is not a limitless supply of everything. We had to be very strict that week and turned away 90% of people who were attending the clinic and we only treated the most severe cases while we were so short of drugs.

With all of the security problems, we needed to have something to lighten the atmosphere, and one of the nicest things which happened that week was the Celebration of Womanhood which was organised by the Jesuit Sisters on Thursday 25th March. It was the first festival which had been organised in the camp since it had been established. CONCERN employees, both expatriate and local staff, were not due any holiday, and so we were meant to work. However, in the event, no women turned up at MCH, and only a handful of very seriously ill people turned up at clinic, so in the end we left a skeleton staff to look after the clinic and hospital and we all had a turn to visit the celebrations.

All of the zones had arranged singing and dancing routines and the display was attended by local dignitaries, United Nations officials, and various NGO personnel. I went with Cyprien, who was very good company, polite, gentle, and quietly friendly. The first dance was a group of men with 'wigs' of very long white hair and bells around their ankles, brandishing bamboo sticks in the air while jumping, swinging, and swaying about to the music. The women were dressed in long red dresses and they sang and waved their hands in the air. There were many displays featuring men, women, and children of all ages, and this was followed by speeches emphasising the importance of women and their work. It was attended by almost all of the refugees from the camp and it was a memorable occasion.

We had to leave the camp early to go back to Kirundo at 2 p.m. for a security meeting. On Wednesday, things seemed to be settling down a bit in Bujumbura, but the news on Thursday was not good as yet again there had been an escalation of violence. Apparently, EC officials were visiting Bujumbura and it was felt that Tutsi extremists had set out to demonstrate that Hutu government did not work. They wanted the officials to witness acts of violence and chaos in the streets. At the security meeting, we were told to prepare for evacuation, in case it became necessary, by ensuring that we had our belongings packed. One of the difficulties which I had to face was telling David that it looked as if he would not be able to travel to Burundi as planned. I didn't feel at all anxious for myself, but I worried constantly about how people felt at home. I sent a fax at David at 7 p.m. and stayed at the Top House for the night to wait for a reply. As there was no way of knowing whether a fax had arrived or not, time seemed to drag by while waiting for an answer. Eventually he telephoned at 9.45 p.m., and as I had expected he was devastated at the news that day, both out of concern for my welfare and at the prospect of not being able to see me as he had planned, which he naturally found very disappointing. Pat had very practically pointed out that we were four hours away from trouble and forty minutes from the nearest border. I was able to say this to David and I think he did find it reassuring.

The following day we had at last had a delivery of drugs from Dublin. The drugs arrived at the camp on Thursday, and the dispensers had to stock up with drugs before the clinic could commence. In African fashion it was done slowly and took most of the morning. Fortunately the clinic was not busy, as the rain was so heavy and it was a very cool day, and this meant that only the very ill made the journey to the clinic from the camp. We did have one funny moment. A rather plump lady came into the clinic, sat down, and proceeded to say that she had lost her appetite. As Cyprien started to interpret it, he saw the funny side of it and started to giggle. We all couldn't help but laugh. We reassured her that she didn't have a problem and we despatched her without drugs or a card for extra rations. She was rather cross about this and stood outside the door scowling at me every time she caught my eye.

We also spent time working on the treatment protocol. I controlled the budget for the Curative Care, for which Andre, the doctor, had no responsibility. He obviously wanted to give everyone the optimum treatment possible. When we looked at the problem from different perspectives, this left areas for discussion and negotiation. For example, we were in a high-risk malarial area. Andre wanted to treat all persons with a temperature with anti-malarial drugs. I knew that if we did this, we would run out of treatment before the next order arrived. So we had to negotiate: if it was a low temperature and no other symptoms, could we wait a day to see what developed rather than treat everybody? We were hoping that one day we would have our own laboratory for blood tests, so that we could confirm malaria *before* treating it, but for the moment there was no way of checking the diagnosis.

Two of our staff were due to get married the following day – Gilbert the hospital cleaner, and Pelagie, one of the clinic drug dispensers. We caught them trying to steal some food from the hospital on the Friday before their Saturday wedding.

They would have to have an official warning on Monday. The UNCHR were making draconian cuts into our budget and we had to take action to try to ensure that the money was spent effectively and not wasted.

When I got back to the house, we had run out of Calor gas for our ring. We normally got this from Bujumbura, but it had not been possible to get supplies because of the situation there. So, instead, we had to get the guards to light a barbecue fire using charcoal every time we wanted to boil a kettle to have a cup of tea or to wash in warm water. Yet another inconvenience to which we had to adjust our lives!

Exodus

The news from Bujumbura was not good. The BBC News said that people were fleeing from Bujumbura to Zaire. On Saturday 25th March *The Daily Telegraph* reported that automatic gunfire and explosions had rocked Bujumbura as the army appeared to be fighting Hutu militias. It was reported that there had been fighting in most areas, including the Buyenzi military base.

It remained very quiet in Kirundo, but we were always hungry for news. People at home were able to pass on reports to us, and also CONCERN from Dublin rang us on the satellite phone for updates several times a day. The general feeling was that at the beginning of the week most of the violence was the result of spontaneous reactions, the main protagonists being the Hutu militia. Towards the end of the week the conflict appeared to be more planned and the Tutsi gangs and army were more implicated. As people started to flee from Bujumbura towards Uvira, Zaire, over the weekend things became quieter. Anne and John were planning to return to Kirundo on Sunday morning, leaving Bujumbura in a convoy for the first part of the journey. Many expatriate staff had left Bujumbura. Many of the NGO workers had moved to Zaire or other quieter parts of Burundi, and a few had left the area altogether.

CONCERN staff at Dublin were obviously extremely jumpy and they had arranged airlifts from Nairobi if the need arose – we had a small airstrip a few miles down the road. Until the previous year, a small aircraft had used to run regular services to Bujumbura, but it had stopped due to security issues. Dublin had also checked which routes we would need to travel on if we evacuated by road.

On Sunday, Pat and I decided to have a dinner party at our house. We had a few luxury items in our cupboard, and Pat thought we might as well eat them up rather than leave them in case we went away and couldn't return. We were really pleased when we heard on the radio that Anne and John were through all of the troubled areas and about one hour's drive away from Kirundo. It was such a relief to us all when they finally arrived. Anne looked really tired and strained and that was hardly surprising. The satellite phone line got very busy after their arrival in Kirundo, as the press at home had got to hear about their ordeal and were ringing up for telephone interviews. David telephoned and told me that he had seen the mass exodus of Burundians who were fleeing to Zaire on the CNN News.

On Monday, the President, Sylvestre Ntibantunganya, told French radio that there were a hundred and fifty dead after the clashes of the past week (*The Independent* 27.3.95). Unofficially, everyone believed the figure was much higher, and many estimated over five hundred. The UNCHR reported that 23,500 had arrived in Uvira, Zaire, of whom about half were returning Zaireans. The government of Zaire in Kinshasa stated that at least two hundred Zaireans had died in the conflict. The violence had reached a peak on Friday night and since then it had started to settle down, although shops and the market were still closed.

Work remained very routine. We were trying to devise a system ensuring that no refugee could get double treatment. At that time anyone who was ill could get treatment at MCH and the clinic. This meant they either took two courses, which could be dangerous, or they could sell one course of tablets in the market. Our work seemed to go on with no alteration from the expected pattern. Perhaps this was as well, as it meant that we didn't have any time to dwell on what might happen if the worst came to the worst.

We had the usual endless security meetings after work, where our view was sought concerning the security. We were told at a meeting on Monday after work that some refugees had been killed in a camp in Ngosi which was a neighbouring province. There were fears that the conflict could escalate during the first week of April as it was the anniversary of the deaths of the presidents of Burundi and Rwanda. As Rob, the Burundi representative was away, Dominic, the Rwandan representative, had arrived to give us some support and to assess the situation.

On Wednesday 29th we attended a meeting at 7.30 a.m. and we were told that we were leaving on Friday 31st for two weeks, travelling to Kigali. Meanwhile, David had heard this from Dublin and had arranged to fly to Kigali to meet me early on Saturday, and from there we were going to travel to Nairobi for a week. The next two days were hectically busy as we had to pack up everything to take with us, as well as ensuring that the camp was fully prepared and had sufficient supplies for two weeks of everything they needed. My responsibility was the pharmacy. Fortunately, I had already been extensively counting the number of drugs prescribed in an average week. This was in order to introduce more control, as there were many indicators that drugs were being stolen and sold in the market. This earlier work had given me a fair idea of the number of drugs needed in the Ruku pharmacy to last for exactly two weeks. The main Kirundo drug store would be completely locked and we would take the keys with us. I also listed inventories of all the equipment so that I could check that it was still there when we returned, then I handed over my responsibilities to various people so that they knew what they had to do while I was away.

Generally, there was a feeling that civil war could be imminent. In *The Independent* on 31st March, it was reported by David Orr that every street contained the burned-out remnants of houses. It was reported in *The Daily Telegraph* on the same day that tens of thousands of refugees were on the move. For at least twelve miles, walking four abreast, on the mountainous roads, were men women and children, heading from camps in Ngosi in northern Burundi to Tanzania. This made it difficult to say goodbye to the people we had come to get to know well in the camp, people who had become our friends. Pat told Cyprien that she had heard of a man who had escaped by dressing as a woman. I gave him my address on an envelope and told him that if I did not come back or he moved, then he must contact me to let me know that he was safe. I said to everyone, "I wish you peace". I started to take some photographs. A soldier came up to me and told me that I could not take photographs as I had not been given permission. Two refugees – Lucien, the pharmacy storekeeper, and Cyprien – were with me so I did not make a fuss as I knew that they could suffer if I did. Instead I put my camera away, and with unspoken tension and an intense feeling of togetherness we walked away from the soldier.

Back at the house we continued our preparations. Pat took charge of the packing and I got food packed ready for the journey. A fax from David had arrived that day to tell me that he was arriving in Kigali on Saturday morning at six o'clock.

On Friday morning we were up at 5.45 a.m.. The cars and people were gathered at the Top House. There were six vehicles and fourteen people to be evacuated: Maddy, Meduoc, Emer, Mike, Andre, Pat and myself from Kirundo, Anne from Bujumbura, Dominic and Peter from Kigali, and Jean, Dominic's driver, John the mechanic and his driver Moussa, and one of our drivers, Janvier, who was planning to work in Rwanda. The new generator had just been fitted and had worked efficiently for two days, before it had to be dismantled and taken back to Rwanda. I was in the car which held the generator, driven by Moussa, who proved to be very good company and an endless source of interesting information.

We loaded the cars and left at 8.30 a.m.. We left Top House at five-minute intervals so that we did not attract attention as we left Kirundo and then regrouped outside the town and travelled in convoy to the border.

Moussa was a Ugandan who spoke very good English. He was a mechanic, married, with a six-year-old daughter called Hafia whom he obviously adored. His chatter was non-stop. As we neared the border, we passed hundreds of half-demolished houses. Moussa said that for each house, a family had been killed. The houses had been homes for Hutu, but now the farms were occupied by Tutsi. We also passed through a refugee camp for Tutsi people, which consisted of a collection of corrugated tin huts. The children did look different to the children in our camp. Their skin seemed darker, and each had a higher forehead, different shaped upper lip, and thinner nose and lips.

We got to the border at 10 a.m.. A few kilometres before the border the farms finished and we drove over scrubland. When we got to the border, Anne collected up passports, and they had to be taken to get an exit stamp. This meant that the details had to be listed in a register – slowly. We had plenty of time to look around. The area around was baked red earth with a few cacti rising up to twelve feet from the ground and a few herbaceous plants with bright yellow daisy-like flowers. The buildings were the usual concrete and metal, two in all, with a flagpole and the red-white-and-green Burundian flag in the middle. Peter made the mistake of leaning against the flag pole and the guards quickly admonished him. The ground was scattered with thousands of tops from beer and Fanta bottles, all trodden into the ground so that they almost formed a pavement. The soldiers in Burundi had worn khaki until about two weeks back, but they had changed to new bright blue uniforms. "Ready for the war," Mike said.

After an hour we all had received our authorisation to leave Burundi and we moved to the Rwandan border at eleven. The border guards were young boys of about twelve to fifteen years old, carrying Kalashnikov rifles. They refused to let us through. Apparently they had been told not to let any refugees into the country, and he did not know whether we were refugees. So they had to radio to Kigali and get an official to come out to meet us. We listened to the news on our radio. Apparently the border between Burundi and Tanzania had closed, trapping Hutu refugees on the border. It was reported that there were 40,000 en route for the Tanzanian border, with 100,000 preparing to leave. We ate our picnic. We played volleyball, read books, sunbathed, and I wrote my diary. We watched the boy soldiers. Apparently they were orphans from the genocide who had no family, and by entering the army they were provided with food and clothing, but no pay. The soldiers played cards immediately in front of us, slapping down the cards, and giggling as all small boys do. They let several cars through while we waited. We knew that we were victims of a power game and if we showed irritation then they had won. So we were patient.

At 3.30 p.m., a man from the Ministry of Defence turned up. He was around thirty years old, with good English, a smart suit, and was escorted by a boy soldier carrying a rifle and a briefcase.

We then drove about 10 minutes to Customs. On this side of the border it is a red-painted corrugated tin hut with IMMIGRATION painted on the door. It took an hour for the passports to be listed again, twice, once by a young man with a smart suit and reasonable English, and once by a boy soldier who wore khaki trousers, a bright tee-shirt, wellingtons, leather jacket and belt. There was much shuffling of passports, which were sorted into arbitrary piles and then sorted again into different piles for some reason which was not apparent. Pat, who was always efficient, became noticeably irritated by the slow progress. Sounding sympathetic, she told the clerk that he was so busy that she would like to help. Her offer was declined. Once we had had all the details recorded, those without visas had to buy them – more forms and twenty dollars – and then we could move from the Immigration Department.

We then had to be searched. Searching at a checkpoint means that everything is removed from each car and every bag or box has to be opened. Meanwhile, the Ministry of Defence man waited for us. At 5 p.m., seven hours after arriving at the border post, we were free to go. The man from the Ministry said he would escort us so that we would not need to be searched again at the checkpoints we would need to pass between the border and Kigali. He drove off at speed.

The journey was over scrubland – I think it's called savannah. The hills here were much more rounded than the hills in Burundi. And then, eventually, farms. Many of the plots were overgrown because their owners and tenants had run away. But some looked as if they had returnees who were trying to weed and tend the land and make it look healthier. We went through a Tutsi town where Moussa told me that thousands of Tutsi had been massacred in the church last year. We crossed a wide river valley with the broad River Nyaberungo meandering along it. We crossed by a single-track metal bridge. Moussa said that the river had hippo, crocodiles, and tricky currents, and in the civil war people had tried to escape by crossing it. Many perished and the river was full of bodies. We reached Kigali eventually at about 7 p.m. and as we entered the town, our escort was waiting for us. We all had to go to the Ministry of Defence for a meeting. We protested, but we were told that this showed a lack of respect for the country, so we had little choice but to follow. But as we arrived at the appropriate building, we were waved on and only Dominic was required to go inside. Apparently, the officials wanted to know why refugees were fleeing from Burundi.

Cuddles In Africa

David arrived on 1st April and we spent one night in Kigali before flying on to Nairobi. Kigali is a beautiful city, sprawling over many hills. One of the CONCERN drivers showed us the sights of the town. There were the usual collection of government buildings, a market and shops, and lots of buildings with bullet-pocking from the genocide and many burnt-out buildings. But Kigali has recovered well. It is bustling, vibrant, colourful, with lots of greenery and ramshackle tin houses stretching as far as the eye can see. We couldn't help but notice the amount of UN cars and the number of NGO offices and cars in Kigali. Someone told us that there are over 150 aid organisations there. We saw the UN soldiers with their light blue insignia, which was a beret, hatband, turban, neckerchief, depending on the nationality of the wearer. Kigali had none of the tension found in Burundi – no gunfire, no grenades, and no curfew. We went out for a very ordinary meal but the enjoyment for us was being with each other, and for me in particular the freedom to travel out of doors at night.

Most of the Kirundo staff were moved out of Kigali over the following week, in case there was trouble at the anniversary of the genocide. They were dispersing to other camps, for example, Pat was doing a nutritional survey with Emer in Goma. David and I caught an early Air Cameroon flight to Nairobi which flew over the vast Lake Victoria. We stayed in the Norfolk Hotel overnight, a gracious and attractive building which seemed to have survived from the colonial days without too much change. Nairobi is full of modern skyscrapers which does not make it particularly interesting. We went shopping. Normally this is not something I like, but it had a novelty value as I had not been near a shop in Burundi and there were a few essential things which I needed.

The following day we went to the Aberdare mountains to stay in a country club. That was real honeymoon stuff! The first night we spent at a game viewing lodge which had a water hole and salt lick. We saw buffalo, elephants, rhino, genet cat, hares and a mongoose, and various types of bush buck. We then spent three nights in a place which was as near to paradise as you could get, especially if you were with someone you loved whom you had not seen for several weeks. The Country Club itself was a grand old character house with a restaurant and bars, with sweeping immaculate lawns spread out in front and surrounded by colourful shrubs. To the left was a view of the Aberdare mountains, in front the wide Rift Valley, and to the right Mount Kenya. The accommodation for guests there was in small individual cottages scattered in the grounds. Ours was on the edge of a wood. We had a large bed-sitting room complete with an open fire, but most important, a bathroom with endless hot water which didn't have to be heated on a charcoal fire.

We walked, talked, laughed, cuddled, and enjoyed each other's company in a haze of happy days. David hired some golf clubs and we were amused at the local rules. If your ball dropped in dung you were allowed a free drop, and if a baboon ran off with your golf ball you were allowed to replace it! David teed off to an audience of guinea fowl, wart hogs, and baboons. We also went on a couple of walks in a game reserve and wandered amongst zebra, giraffe, antelope, and one lovely ostrich. We sunbathed and relaxed in the gardens and then went back to Kigali via Nairobi after one week away.

We still didn't know whether the team would return to Kirundo. The news had been mixed while we had been away. Bujumbura was quieter, but there were reports of atrocities in the north. In Mayinga province there had been reports of Hutu rounded up in their villages and massacred, although there were widely different estimations of the numbers concerned. More seriously from our own personal welfare, there were two expatriate journalists killed on the road between Bujumbura and Kirundo, and once again it appeared that they were targets rather than caught in crossfire.

When we returned to Kigali one week after leaving it, we stayed in a flat near the town centre overlooking the hills with green fields, winding red roads and thousands of tin shacks in front of us. When we awoke, we heard the sound of people, the babbling of voices and the tramping of feet as they walked to school, work and market. We saw people crowding streets and we enjoyed people-watching. We saw a hairdresser in a tin hut trimming hair, a crowd of women all with colourful clothes, and in front of them a cloth on which they placed their wares for sale – a few bananas or onions. A small stall spread out with items such as soap and sweets, and two young Muslim salesgirls sitting underneath the stall so that they could keep out of the heat of the sun. A sign saying SUPER BUTCHER with the remains of the carcass of a goat hung up in the full sun, and every time a customer appeared the butcher would pull out his huge machete and chop a bit off. We saw a pygmy pushing a huge laden cart up a steep hill and wondered why such an arduous task seemed to fall on such a little fellow.

It was peaceful in Kigali, but the prisons were full of people awaiting trials, and all around Kigali were purple banners asking the international community to support justice and retribution for the perpetrators of the genocide in 1994.

A Misunderstanding Explained

When David arrived in Kigali, he was anxious and strained. We had done lots of thinking and talking; he was happy now. One of the problems which we had to face was that NGO are usually paternalistic organisations which have no choice but to please their sponsor. When they faced a situation they had not faced before, the people who made decisions felt uncertain and defensive. They had not employed a wife and mother with a devoted and loving husband at home before. We did not, and would not, pose a security risk but we were an unknown entity to CONCERN and they reacted with total caution. This had created a great deal of stress for us. One example of this was David's trip to Kigali. Apparently, when David knew that I was to be evacuated to Kigali, he discussed this with someone at the head office who said that there would be no problem if David flew to Kigali to meet me. There were no objections to travelling in Rwanda by the Foreign Office at the time either, so David booked his ticket. After this, CONCERN telephoned David and told him not to go to Kigali, but as the ticket had already been bought, he told them that he did not intend to change his plans because they had changed their minds, unless there was a very good reason.

What particularly annoyed him was that when he arrived in Kigali another CONCERN employee had his nineteen-year-old son visiting him at the same time and no objections whatsoever had been raised to this. We have three teenage children who are competent and sensible, but we also know for certain that David's experience of life and extremely sensible nature would make him a much better risk if an emergency arose. We therefore felt that David had suffered unfair discrimination and in many ways felt this to be demeaning.

At Christmas, an employee of CONCERN had a boyfriend from home visiting her. There was a crisis and he, together with the team, were evacuated to Kigali. After the crisis he returned to Kirundo with the rest of the team. There were precedents set therefore for David to return to Kirundo with me, following an evacuation to Kigali. David is a totally stable person: calm, gentle, and well-organised by nature, mature and sensible, and the sort of person that everyone relies on. Nothing in his character or history would have made people feel that he was a security risk.

When I had written home, I had pointed out the problems for student refugees in Rwanda as they could not continue with their studies. David was a governor of a local college of further education. He discussed this as an issue with the head of the college, who put him in touch with the World University Service. Between them they had come to realise that the biggest problem would be getting exit visas. David had offered to go to Africa to do this. In many ways he found this really appealing. He knew that I was having an exciting adventure and was doing something worthwhile. He also wanted to do something on which he could put his stamp and he saw this as a chance, a scheme of his own that he had discovered for himself, and as far as he knew, he would be the only person doing it. The possibility made him really excited. When he discussed this with CONCERN staff at Kigali, the assumption was that he was making out that he was interested in doing this as an excuse to be with me. The response was that if he worked in Rwanda or Burundi, then I could not continue in CONCERN's employment. This created yet more frustration in him. We were in love, but we had never lived in each other's pockets. I had spent a year away from home at university without it causing any problems. Because he knew where I was and that I was safe, he didn't even bother to telephone me most weeks, and I didn't worry if he didn't. Often we chose to have separate weekends and holidays; we worked together and lived together and we both enjoyed a change of company. But now that I was in Africa, David felt a sense of envy that I was having fun while he was trapped at home. He wanted and needed to do something for himself as much as I wanted to do something for myself. This message somehow could not get through to the people who made decisions for CONCERN.

It was decided that the CONCERN team would return to work in Kirundo on Wednesday 12th April. David's return ticket was dated 17th April. It seemed a reasonable request to ask if he could return to Kirundo with me. The answer was no. To say that David was disappointed was a serious understatement. He also needed to feel that CONCERN the organisation, was on his side, respected him, and did not view him as an idiot. It also made me feel incredibly frustrated with the situation. I wanted to work for CONCERN and I felt certain that I could do a good job. I knew that if CONCERN continued to discriminate so personally against him in particular, he would feel so cross that it would be difficult for me to continue in a job I really wanted to do and thought I could do well. There was absolutely no one who would listen to our point of view. I think it was the lack of trust, dialogue, and understanding between CONCERN and David which created more problems than the actual separation.

On Tuesday 11th, our last night, David and I stayed in a mediocre but expensive hotel in Kigali. We then had an ordinary meal in a rooftop restaurant overlooking the hills of Kigali. The houses did not have electricity and the only lights were small sparkling street lights at intervals, dotted across the whole vista. It was like looking at a fairyland. It should have been romantic, but instead we felt flat and without emotion. We decided to say our goodbyes that night so that the next day we would not have an emotional farewell.

The next morning the land cruiser arrived. We said our farewells, and after a quick hug I walked away and got into the car. I was off to Kirundo. David was going to try to get an early flight home.

Kirundo Again

We had an uneventful journey. Pat and I unpacked and we sorted out our house. Pat was angling all the time to get a car to get to the camp. The problem was that this was the season of the 'big rains', and the combination of lorries and rains along the narrow dirt track to the camp had apparently made it impassable. We were invited to the local bar called the Democrat for a drink, but Pat and I declined. We wanted to get some preparation done for returning to the camp the following day.

That evening I had my first real doubt that Kirundo was where I should be. I loved every minute of living in Kirundo and I loved my job. But I imagined David, lonely in Kigali, and I thought that was where my first duty lay.

We could not drive along my favourite enchanting route to work, and instead we took a longer and not so pretty route across scrubland and arrived at the camp from the opposite direction. This time we could see the camp in the distance as we approached it, the blue *blunde* stretching across the hills. It was wonderful to meet everyone again. They were so thrilled to see us and also they wanted to demonstrate to us that they had managed everything well while we were away. We were thrilled to see that they were all still at the camp and to catch up with news of old friends. There was much to do. Almost at once I was meeting with Tharcisse to find out what progress he had made in organising the registration scheme.

There was also a meeting set up with Roger, who was the United Nations representative at the camp, and four people who were educated to undergraduate or graduate level. There had been more, but the camp had been raided during the previous year in November and most of the educated Hutu had been removed and not seen again. The four included Cyprien, Charles from Therapeutic, a water plant worker, and a teacher. All that Roger could offer was a room for cultural and educational opportunities. He stressed that although there was a secondary school for girls in Kirundo and a university in Bujumbura, the security situation made it impossible to guarantee the safety of any Hutu student who went there.

Meanwhile, the day had turned very cold and wet. The rain had to be seen to be believed. It poured – too fast to soak into the ground or to run across the ground into the drains. Instead it formed a layer of water across the whole earth. Walking in it for just a few minutes I had got soaked to the skin and very cold. Pat found a priest who was returning to Kirundo and organised a lift for me. He dropped me off at the office in Kirundo. In a few moments Mike turned up, and with a big smile announced that David was in Kirundo. I could hardly believe it! I jumped in the car and went back to the house, to find myself rushing up to a triumphant and grinning David, who had hired a car to come to visit me.

The best thing was that he looked happy. He could only stay for an hour, as he had a return ticket to Brussels the following day. Maddy insisted that he had a Codan car to take him back to Kigali, so David's hire car and driver followed the CONCERN car. Maddy wasn't pleased, but *I* was. I hoped that this would make David feel a sense of satisfaction, a feeling that he had somehow made a statement. I hoped this would make him better able to accept my work in Kirundo, and if he could, then I could stay. I went to bed with my new cassette with all of my favourite records which David had brought from England with him as a present. I kept finding myself smiling when I didn't know I was, my face just mirroring the contentment of my mind.

I knew that it would confirm in the minds of CONCERN managers that David was an irresponsible and unpredictable security risk and that they had been right all along. However, this seemed to be the intractable view that they had of him before the incident – nothing had been lost there. David had tried all of the reasonable channels first and had been denied. There is nothing as frustrating as seeing your position as lose-lose. Perhaps one day, wives and mothers working overseas will be a more common occurrence. Being one of the first, I've set the ball rolling and started decision-makers in non-government organisations thinking. Unfortunately, someone has to be the first, and the trend setters have to battle for any privileges – it's the way of the world.

There were a few grenades in Kirundo that night. Apparently, the prime minister of Burundi was visiting the province so it was in his honour, perhaps to make him feel at home. But, according to staff on the bus to work the next day, no damage was done.

The Old Team And The New Team

It's easy to think that a small expatriate team in a hostile environment tackling a difficult task would get on incredibly well together. But just like in any other working situations, tensions arose.

Our team leader was Maddy and she had a hard time when faced with Pat and myself. We were both strong-minded individuals, Pat with thirteen years tropical medicine experience, and myself with the same number of years experience in management of care. Sometimes there were stresses between Pat and myself, but we were both determined not to argue with each other, but to look at issues as they arose, and up to that point we had overcome any problems. Maddy saw us as a team, and I would be surprised if she didn't feel threatened by us.

Mike was sensible, practical and lovely, and he got on with his job. Meduoc was a very gentle character, who tended to take a background role. Andre was difficult to communicate with at first as he spoke French, although over the weeks his English improved as did our French, so we communicated better. Emer didn't really have any female of her own age to whom she could relate except Maddy, and they weren't really on the same wavelength. Yet between us we had an immense amount of skill and ability. We were a collection of talented individuals rather than a terrific team, and we often pulled away from each other rather than pulling with each other, not because we didn't like and respect each other, but just because we didn't seem to be focused and united.

You can't choose the people that you constantly live with and work with in that sort of situation. You might be lucky and find someone you can relate to easily. The teams change every few weeks – someone leaves and someone new comes. The constant change of personnel puts further strain on people and on relationships. Your close friends at home are not people that you have met in the last few weeks: they are people that you have known for months or years. They are selected as friends from a large pool of people, the ones with whom you are most compatible. When you are with people you have only known a few weeks, if you have something which really distresses you, you can only confide in them so many times. Everyone has a limit to the time they can listen to other people's problems. So individuals away from home and family often store within them their own personal problems and cope with them in their own way. Many people who work overseas are single people. They might decide to move overseas at a period of change in their lives – the end of a relationship, the loss of a job. There are not many people in happy, long-term, supportive relationships – the sort of relationships which help us to cope in difficult times – and this is the opposite of "real" society in any culture. When you have a long-term relationship with a partner or a long-term friend, you know that they will accept you and listen to you, however stupid and silly you may seem. Recruitment of partners, especially long-term partners, is not the norm when filling overseas positions, although VSO are the one group who seem to be able to appreciate and accommodate the stability that this can give to a project. In a stressful work situation such as Burundi, my own view is that mature people in long-term partnerships would be better able to cope with the stress of the living and working environment because the partners would be able to understand and support each other.

Boredom is another huge problem. With irregular electricity, occasional videos only, curfew, few people to mix with, coping with free time when you are meant to be relaxing can be seen as daunting. Some people who work for NGO seemed to have a big problem with drinking – not social drinking and the occasional night, when too much is imbibed, but regular, nightly, heavy drinking. This doesn't mean that we all went about arguing and getting drunk. It means, however, that there are constant tensions in living overseas which add to the stress of the job and different people have different ways of relieving it.

Our team was due to be split up soon after the return from Kigali. Maddy was leaving, as was Mike, Meduoc wanted a transfer to Tanzania, and Andre was due to return to Togo. There was much gossip among the team about who was to fill the vacancy of team leader. Eventually this job was taken by an engineer called Padraig who was to become team leader and engineer. We had a Scot called Jim, who took over the engineering job, when Mike left, for three weeks and then moved on to Tanzania. Emer was to take over the logistician's work as well as the administrative work. The expatriate team was getting smaller as more and more responsibility was being given to local employees.

The arrival of a new team leader put a new vitality into the team and we felt that we were more focused and pulled together better. Padraig did not speak French and he needed Emer to go to all meetings with him to translate, which made her job more interesting. He tended to delegate more, and everyone's job developed a deeper and more interesting component. Pat was taking on more responsibility in the Health Education Department and the supplementary feeding unit. I was continuing my work on pharmacy and clinic controls.

One thing happened, which really surprised me at the time and eventually caused me quite a few headaches. Before Maddy left, I was asked to be the health coordinator. It was the last thing I had expected, as Pat and Andre had so much more experience than me in health care in Africa. It meant taking over the administration of the health team. I suppose if it had been something I had considered as a possibility, I would have asked more questions, but, as it was, I was so surprised that I just accepted it. I wished later that I had insisted that it had first been cleared with Pat and Andre. As it was, nothing was said to them, and it was left to me to tell them what I had been asked to do.

It was probably the best possible option. Andre and Pat had an excellent knowledge of tropical diseases. I had more experience of management and administration, and therefore it was using our skills to best advantage. The difficulty which I had to overcome was that Pat understandably saw my appointment as a personnel slight, and it made her feel very low and depressed, as well as angry and misunderstood. There were other problems in my relationship with Andre which unfolded over the next few weeks.

Maddy's leaving do was on the 21st April. It had to be before curfew and so it started at 2 p.m. and went on until 7 p.m., but that made little difference, as Africans are good at having fun at any time. We had the party in our house because it was the largest house. The expatriate staff from other NGO were invited, as well as some of the local officials and the staff who worked for CONCERN in the office and the camp. The house staff worked very hard to provide a very good spread of food and we put on the generator and fixed up loud music, and the event went very well. From my point of view, it gave me a good opportunity to talk to Tharcisse on a personal level and find out more about his background and family. Tharcisse and his family had moved from Burundi to Rwanda because of ethnic conflicts, and Tharcisse had to return to Burundi to work because he could not find work in Rwanda. We had always got on very well at work, but from this point, our working relationship improved as we understood each other better when we knew more about our backgrounds. We had started to overcome the cultural divide and learn from each other.

Pat was upset because of my new appointment. She was also upset because of the party. Large parties with lots of people were not Pat's favourite events, although she loved to organise smaller social events such as dinner parties. But these social events, in what she rightly viewed as her home, she liked to control herself, and this was organised by CONCERN office staff. By comparison I felt much more content. David had telephoned in the week and he was obviously happier after his African adventure. I felt challenged by the new role which I had been offered and I was looking forward to doing administration and management because it is what I do best.

Whereas previously Pat and I had always talked easily even about our differences and I had found her very supportive when I had problems, when it came to my turn to support Pat I found that she was less good at receiving than she was at giving. She was a generous person who liked to be in control and to help others. She saw being upset as a failing and felt that she had to bear it alone or with prayer, and when I offered her empathy she saw it as pity, which of course she didn't want. So talking, once easy, became an impossibility, and there was a big divide between us.

One further problem which made life stressful had to be the reduced opportunities to mix with and make new friends in the local communities. Due to the security situation, there were curfews which were socially restricting. But also, in a country full of ethnic tensions, all people had to be careful with whom they mixed. You never want to be associated with someone who might, for whatever reason, be seen as the wrong type. This restriction applied to Burundians and expatriates alike. Getting it wrong could have a penalty which cost you your life.

But Padraig was determined that we would start to gel as a team. The first weekend he was in Kirundo he arranged for us all to have an outing to a place called Kigosi. It was a small settlement on the edge of the lake. A group of nuns ran a small guesthouse, beerhouse and restaurant. We arrived on Sunday lunchtime. Although it was warm, the skies were overcast, and the lake, silver and shimmering, stretched out into the distance, the lush green vegetation grew down to the edge of the lake. The only other diners at the restaurant were a group of soldiers at the next table. We asked what food was available. We were told omelettes, salad, and chips. That was what we ordered. Half an hour later we heard that they had no eggs. We had salad and chips and washed it down with beer. It took an hour to prepare lunch for us all. But just sitting and talking as a group, rather than all doing our own thing in our own houses, was a worthwhile experience and I think everyone enjoyed the change.

Work And The Security Situation

It was busy in the health care section of the camp towards the end of April because of the "big rains". Everywhere was a red mud bath, and life in a *blunde* was not fun. Apart from the wetness and humidity, it was difficult or impossible to keep clean, and in consequence there was an outcrop of disease. Amongst these particularly were chest infections, which seemed to affect small children most of all; diarrhoea increased significantly; malaria was increased because the puddles of water encouraged mosquitoes; and there was a huge outbreak of conjunctivitis. The clinics were hectic. We tried to spread the workload. Pat took all the under twos for consultation at MCH, and all of the people with diarrhoea were sent straight to the dysentery unit. We arranged with the Health Education to hold clinics for people with conjunctivitis. Even so, the clinics were full of very sick people every day, and the hospital in-patients had risen from about six or eight to thirty or more, with some people lying on mats in the middle of the ward. In the dysentery unit, the staff had no alternative but to allocate two people to lie on each bed.

On the political front it was now quieter in Burundi, but Rwanda was having its turn at grabbing world headlines. A displaced persons camp in Kibeho which in the south of Rwanda, was forcibly closed down. Apparently the UN had made an undertaking to resettle people from this camp into their own homes, but nothing had happened. The Rwandan government finally lost patience and sent in the army to disperse the people who lived there. One hundred and ten thousand displaced Hutus were forced to gather in a restricted area and then the soldiers opened fire. Estimates of the numbers killed varied from eight thousand (initial figures given by United Nations) to three hundred (the official Rwandan government statistic). The displaced people soon concluded that they would very much like to go home as quickly as possible. Rob, the country representative from Bujumbura, went there to assess the situation, and the reception centre run by CONCERN in Ndere in Kigali was involved in resettlement. Two displaced children's camps in Rwanda were also involved, as any children who had become separated from their families were taken there.

This really was very much Pat's speciality, as there were very few people who were as experienced as her. So she offered her services if needed in Rwanda while there was a short-term crisis in Rwanda. She left Kirundo on Friday 28th, looking forward to the challenge in Rwanda.

The rains had made deliveries to the camp difficult. Two food lorries got stuck in the mud and were looted, so there was a shortage of ration at distribution. The rains also meant that we couldn't get our washing dried. Our clothes got covered in mud at work and my shoes and jeans needed to be changed every day. The problem at the time was that the housemaid couldn't get my clothes dry. Coming home one day to find two pairs of ironed jeans waiting for me was an immense relief and gave me a great deal of pleasure. Yet, despite all its frustrations, Africa has a special magic of its own and I loved being there.

The week after Maddy left there were a large number of significant changes, which became my problem, as the health coordinator. As the only nurse left in the camp, I now had direct responsibility for about two hundred staff and had to deal with problems in the clinic, day hospital, dysentery unit, therapeutic and supplementary feeding units, health education, and maternal and child health. I also had to find what I needed to do in my new administrative post. Various statistics had to be sent to the United Nations. I had to find what information they needed, where to find it from, decide where and how to record it.

One of the changes was linked to the treatment of TB. In the past, no treatment had been available for TB sufferers in the camp. The logic behind this was that transient populations were not likely to be able to complete a course of treatment which would continue for a year, and part treatment would lead to resistance against TB drugs. There seemed to be a recent change in the attitudes towards this at the World Health Organisation, and now it was decided that TB treatment could be given.

In fact, CONCERN had already been treating TB cases, even though funding was not given by the UN or WHO. The rationale behind this was that if a small number of cases were untreated, eventually, because of living conditions, the disease would spread. If and when treatment was funded, the costs would be much higher. Any cases we suspected were sent to the local hospital in Kirundo, where refugees were admitted to a unit there for a few weeks and then returned to the camp. After this we had to obtain treatment from the hospital through a member of staff fetching drugs every week and distributing them. Paying for this service from the local hospital was extremely expensive and used up a lot of the health budget, and so reducing reliance on Kirundo by providing our own TB care was seen as cost-effective.

Maddy told me this information in her hand-over, and from here began a mammoth search for information and drugs. First of all I contacted Anne in Bujumbura, who in turn contacted the WHO there, as Maddy had said that they had two hundred doses of TB drugs for us. I was told that the drugs had been sent to Kirundo Hospital. To visit Kirundo I had to have a different interpreter – Cyprien was not allowed from the camp. So I took the office manager, called Alexis. I was introduced to a man who was apparently in charge of the hospital. He knew nothing. He did not know if there was a TB protocol. The doctor in charge of TB patients was away, and he didn't know when he would return. The nurse who looked after TB patients couldn't be seen either because, this being Friday afternoon, she had left for the weekend. The pharmacy couldn't be opened because there was no pharmacist in the hospital. Eventually, we negotiated that if I sent a car to fetch the pharmacist, he would arrange to open the pharmacy.

MSF provided many of the drugs in the hospital. Although they had left the area once, they had been considering whether to continue with their project because of the security issues, and had decided to return and continue with a smaller team. There were two pharmacies in the hospital – a Kirundo hospital pharmacy where we obtained a few drugs such a vaccines, and an MSF pharmacy. The Kirundo hospital pharmacy had a very small supply of drugs, and the pharmacist who turned up had the keys to the MSF pharmacy. I thought it was very unlikely that CONCERN drugs would be in there, but I looked, and there weren't any. It seemed like a wasted afternoon.

With Alexis I decided to look around the hospital. What a sight! There was broken equipment, beds with mattresses stolen, and patients lying on the springs. Everywhere was dirty. I was glad to have seen it. It made our day hospital, with its wooden bench-type beds made in the camp, seem very attractive by comparison and it helped me put our care into an African perspective.

The delay in leaving the hospital proved to be useful. I had thought that I would leave without any information. But the French MSF team arrived at the hospital and at least they were able to answer questions. They assured me there *was* a protocol for TB treatment. I could get a copy by asking for 'Com', who had already left to begin his weekend, but I could see him the following week.

I then met a man selling a microscope. I had heard a rumour that there could be one for sale at the hospital via Maddy. We badly needed a microscope at the camp for testing our specimens, particularly for malaria. I checked it and it seemed okay. So I decided that I would report my find to Padraig and see if we could take the risk in purchasing it. The risk was whether or not we were purchasing stolen property belonging to the hospital. I found that the hospital inventory listed three microscopes and I was shown four, which demonstrated that the hospital held one microscope which was not on its inventory. Taking all of the details, I said that I would let him know.

A huge problem emerged in a big way during the week, although we had been given some forewarning that something was likely to happen. Pat and I had been doing some research in preparation. Earlier I had referred to the way that money was paid for refugees. Our funding at CONCERN came from donor nations via United Nations. The world was no longer as sympathetic towards Rwanda and its intractable problems; other countries had their share of media coverage, and funding for Rwandans was drying up. The United Nations was left with huge numbers of Rwandan refugees who resisted all attempts to repatriate them to their homeland and were given less and less money to support them. We were finally given new pay scales for refugees and Burundian staff. Whereas in the past we knew that we would have to cut the number of staff but we were not sure exactly to what level, now the numbers allowed and funded were actually specified.

In getting ready for the expected reductions, Pat and I had been writing job descriptions and looking where cuts could be made in our departments. In some places it was obvious that the demand had dropped and so fewer staff were needed. For example, when the camp was set up, a large number of starving people entered into it and in consequence there were large numbers of staff employed in therapeutic and supplementary feeding. The level of nutrition in the camp was now good, although planned cuts in the basic ration could alter this in the future, so staff were under-utilised in these departments. There were other statements by the United Nations which had to be specifically followed. For example, the UN had said that the Traditional Birth Attendants should not be paid. These ladies had previously worked in Pat's department – some were superb and some were dreadful. In their own communities in Rwanda, these people assisted with childbirth for a small fee or a present. The UN felt that if they were being paid, this was something which they would not get in their own community and it had to stop. There were also areas where we needed to increase staff. An example of this was the possibility of setting up a new TB unit which had not existed previously.

While doing job descriptions, it made me look critically at what responsibilities staff had. I came across a lot of anomalies. For example, in the clinic, only qualified nurses or the doctor could prescribe drugs. However, in Therapeutic and Dysentery, unit drugs were prescribed sometimes by people who had only had a few months experience. This not only led to over-prescribing but also to mistakes. For example, a small child with severe anaemia was prescribed an antibiotic called Chloramphenicol. It was Pat's opinion that the child did not need antibiotics at all, but worse was the *choice* of antibiotic. Chloramphenicol could depress the bone marrow function and aggravate the anaemia. Other examples were overdosage of worming tablets, which caused the child's stomach pain, anorexia and diarrhoea, which was then mistaken as further evidence of worms, and so more anti-worming medication given! We needed to be specific about drugs which only the doctor could prescribe, for example, antibiotics for venereal diseases, drugs which qualified nurses could prescribe, and drugs which trained auxiliaries could prescribe, for example, vitamins, scabies treatment, and simple pain relieving drugs. If we were going to expect trained auxiliaries to prescribe these, there *had* to be a training plan.

Pat had been looking into the work in the Health Education Department. This was a department where the staff taught health in the camp, a bit like health visitors, but without qualifications except on-the-job training given by their supervisor. The UN had made specific recommendations: we needed one health educator to every five hundred people in the camp. We had a few too many, perhaps ten or so, so some had to be made redundant. We didn't know any of the staff, and if we had asked the two supervisors (one a refugee, one a Burundian) to make a choice, they could make choices based on threats, family links, or bribes. So Pat had set about making a written test so that the choice would be a fair one. She asked one supervisor called Leonard for a list of the subjects he had taught to the health workers, and from this she devised a few questions. These were then translated into the local language, as some of the health workers did not speak French, by Cyprien, who was sworn to secrecy, and typed in the office in Kirundo by a typist also sworn to secrecy. Pat had also arranged with Leonard the date of the test. We had also decided to retain three birth attendants as specialist health workers and had asked Vincent, the technical assistant in her department, to devise a verbal test as not all of the midwives could write. This was the stage she had reached when she went to Rwanda.

One of the really unfair things which we did not like were the pay scales which were imposed. Up until that point in time, refugees and Burundians were paid the same rate for the same job. This may have been unfair to Burundians, because they did not have housing and food provided and the refugees did. The new pay scales, however, were strongly biased the other way, with Burundians being paid some four times the amount earned by refugees. My workers in the health department consisted of approximately 20% Burundians, who were in the main Tutsi, and 80% Hutu refugees. Although Burundians had to be employed in the office in Kirundo, in no one else's department were so many Burundi people employed at a basic level. So anomalies were going to be evident and they also were likely to fall along ethnic divisions, with Tutsis being paid more. It was likely to cause a conflict situation. For example, in the dressing room the head of the unit was a refugee called Jean who would earn 10,000 BF per month (400=£1). His two Burundian assistants whom he had trained would earn 32,000 BF per month. One of the decisions, which would be mine, was who was to be made redundant and who was to stay. If in the main I made all of the local staff, Burundian and probably Tutsi, working in basic unskilled jobs redundant, would I be seen as favouring Hutus and could this make me a target and put me at risk? These were the sort of issues I had to grapple with in my first week as health coordinator.

There was also the first sign of problems between myself and Andre. He was an excellent doctor and, I thought, a great teacher. He was an extrovert who liked an audience. He worked hard. In the hospital and the clinic he was constantly following up the work of staff, talking to staff about illnesses and treatment. Everyone liked and respected him, and so did I.

On Wednesday evening at the health meeting, Padraig asked for an organogram of the health department so that he could start to understand it better, and I agreed to do one. I did one that night and gave it to Padraig on Thursday morning. Later that day, Padraig called a meeting with the managerial staff of all of the health departments at the camp, because we now had notification of the imposed cuts from the UN, and he wanted to involve all of the managers. He brought out my organogram to show to people and asked for their comments. Andre immediately decided that I had not put him in the place where he wanted to be. This resulted in a very personal attack on me, saying that I did not show him respect and did not understand his job and made decisions without consulting him. He went on to say that I would not treat a white doctor the same way. I was a bit shocked as I was not expecting it. Whenever we had talked, usually via an interpreter, I'd thought that Andre liked me as much as I liked him. That didn't mean we hadn't done some hard negotiating, where we had looked at things like the protocol from different viewpoints, but I didn't think that the views expressed then were anything other than professional negotiations which had ended amicably.

On leaving work that day, Tharcisse stopped me. With a smile he asked me if I knew why Andre did not like me. I said that perhaps I had misunderstood the relationships and roles of the nurse and doctor in Africa and had offended him because of it. Tharcisse said that the reason was because it was strongly rumoured that I was going to make his mistress redundant. It was said in a mischievous and gossipy way, naming a sixteen-year-old Burundian receptionist from the day hospital. I couldn't believe it and thought Tharcisse had it wrong. So I just gave Tharcisse a look which dismissed the conversation and put the thought to the back of my mind.

I loved my job and I had Burundi-itis – I was totally absorbed and fascinated by its politics and culture. I wanted to stay more than anything else. I was just beginning to feel my feet and starting to understand what I could and should do to be most effective. I had just started to be able to speak a bit of simple French and I could quite often understand what was said to me if people spoke slowly and clearly. I was beginning to build good relationships with the people in the camp and learn the strengths and weaknesses of each employee, finding whom I could depend on and who needed help to develop to their full potential.

But it was at this time that I decided to hand in my notice and leave at the end of three months instead of staying out my six-month contract. David and CONCERN seemed to be involved in a power struggle, and I was 'piggy in the middle'. I couldn't persuade David to accept the situation, because he felt trapped by home and, like me, he wanted to be doing something exciting, different and worthwhile. I couldn't persuade CONCERN that David would not in any way be a security threat. David had initially seemed to be more content when he first returned from his African adventure, but now it was obvious when I spoke to him that he would not be happy while I remained in Africa. I had been put into a situation of having to choose, and my first loyalty was to my family ties.

I had a heavy cold. My bedroom leaked badly in the rain, and the floor was constantly full of puddles. I couldn't get my clothes washed and dried, and often I had to go to work in mud-splattered clothes and come home in damp clothes as I had been caught in the rain. Pat had gone to Rwanda, and I felt that we did not part in as friendly a way as I had wanted and I felt upset because of it. Andre for some reason didn't like what I was doing. I had to leave a job which I loved and which stimulated me, and stretched my skills and imagination in a hundred ways. It was a time when I indulged in a bit of self-pity. But even as I did, I knew that I was luckier than most, especially the refugees who had no bright future at all. Rob, the country representative, came to Kirundo on 28th April, and I handed in my notice to leave at to leave at the end of May.

Saturday was busy, as both Pat and I had planned a very full day, and also Andre had a weekend away in Bujumbura. So with Pat and Andre away, I had to do the work of three people. One of the important things was administering Pat's test, which she had planned for the health workers. There were so many things to get through single handed that I had to ask one of the local Burundian nurses to help me. I chose Angele. I thought she made good judgments, although she was not always liked by the expatriate team members. She didn't smile often and she had an abrupt manner. When I asked her to help me keep an eye on things and do some of the things which normally would be done by myself and Andre, such as the hospital round and discharges, she was really pleased. She coped well and I thought that this had helped me to start building up a relationship with her which would develop in a very positive way.

Communications

In England I could walk or drive to visit friends when I wanted to, pick up the telephone, and rely on it working, write a letter and post it and feel annoyed if it didn't arrive by next day's post. You took it for granted. Communication in this part of Africa was quite different. You had to be prepared to try, try, and try again, and perhaps still not succeed. This was as difficult locally, because of the language and curfew, as it was internationally. You had to adjust to making a plan, executing it with time, effort and detail, and at the end of it be prepared to shrug your shoulders if the plan didn't work.

Towards the end of April our satellite phone and fax gave up working. It was going to be some time before we could get them repaired. Anne radioed from Bujumbura. David had telephoned there and said that there was a possibility of a place at college for Cyprien through the World University Service, but we had to be really quick to get it organised as applications closed the following May. David wanted to come out to Africa to deal with it himself but was not given permission.

Rob was helpful and arranged for me to use the UN telephone in Ngosi the following day. We left Kirundo at 7.45 a.m.. It would take us about one hour to get there. Ngosi is on the road to Bujumbura and there were some big refugee camps there run by MSF Belgium. The weather was extremely wet, and overnight there had been some thunderstorms.

We arrived at the UN at 9 a.m.. After trying to make a phone call without success we went on to MSF and asked if we could use their telephones. It transpired that all of the telephones in Ngosi had been knocked out by the thunderstorm the previous night. So after that we had no choice but to go on to Bujumbura if I was to make the call. This was the road on which two journalists had been killed two weeks before and it was meant to be out of bounds to all CONCERN staff except Rob. It was extremely peaceful that day. As we drove towards Bujumbura again we could feel the heat as we descended, and once we were there the weather improved and it was hot and sunny. We couldn't waste time because we had to return to Kirundo before the curfew. We ate, I spoke to Anne about the TB drugs, I spoke to David on the phone, and he faxed out the details for us to fill in. The good news was that Cyprien could get a place at Norton Radstock College but that was only a start – there were so many obstacles, it was only the beginning of a dream. The good news for David, of course, was that I would be home at the end of May.

We got back to Kirundo at 5.30 p.m., and except for a quick lunch break, nearly ten hours travelling had been necessary in order for me to make one telephone call. We met everyone at the Democrat for a Primus beer and then went back to the Top House where everyone watched a video and I wrote my diary and thought about the things I had seen in the day on my journey, things which were typical of Burundi and which I would like to always remember.

One of the interesting things which I read recently was an account of the way Africans carry things on their heads. Apparently, women in Africa don't use any more energy when they carry large loads in this way, compared with being unladen. The reason is because they carry weight through their *bones*, whereas we use bone and muscle. If Europeans carried the same weight on their heads, they would be more liable to a neck injury.

The items people carry are really interesting to see, and as I was bring driven along the road it was always a point of interest to look at the loads. There are always the usual baskets with fruit and vegetables. Often people carry items such as beans, rice and maize flour in bags or sacks on their heads, tied at the top with an elaborate knot, and looking like a huge wide sun hat shading the wearer from the weather. Wood can be in any shape, from a bundle of twigs to a large log, or a long tree trunk perhaps twelve feet in length, swaying gently as the bearer saunters gracefully along the road. There are small bits of furniture such as stools, jerrycans full of water, square oil cans, huge piles of tea leaves or tobacco which drape so much over the front and back that you have to wonder how he or she can see where to walk. There are crates with twelve large bottles of beer, cooking pots with unknown contents, a machete, a banana leaf acting as sunshade or rainshade, depending on the weather, a rolled-up umbrella, a chicken in a string bag. The list was endless, and I found myself continually trying to spot something I had not seen before.

Another common sight was people chopping at fallen trees. Where trees had fallen beside the road, people sat astride the tree, chopping it with axe and machete, and there would be a line of local people transporting it bit by bit along the road on their heads. Wood is important in Africa – it is the *only* fuel. I described the use for it in the camp for cooking and the people who carried it along the road. It came as a shock to me to learn how important wood is to the economy in rural Africa. Of course, when you think about it, it is obvious and logical. In places like Burundi, where most people existed by subsistence farming, towns were relatively small. Some of the largest collections of people were in the refugee camps. This might be true also in bigger countries like Zaire and Tanzania. This put an enormous strain on the local area and ecology. Refugees needed trees and they had no alternative but to chop them down. Around camps there was a noticeable absence of trees. Also, just chopping them down presented an ethical dilemma. I spoke to a Red Cross employee who was talking about his work, which included making decisions about how to organise wood for fuel in camps. The choice was whether to use local workers and traditional methods of axe and machete, or to buy two-man saws. With two-man saws, a tree could be chopped up in a sixth of the time, saving money, and the idea of economical use of time would be taught to a developing nation. Using traditional methods, men were paid, were kept occupied, and felt that they had a useful role in society.

Other interesting discussions I had in Africa with other expatriate staff included the collection of water. Women traditionally collected water. Sometimes they had to walk miles and they returned with the cans on their heads. The aid workers' answer was to provide a well in the village. But women worked all day. Going for a walk with a friend to a nearby lake or to a well in a neighbouring village was time off for them – a social time. It was *not* a chore. Providing a water pump in the village meant that the children fetched the water and the women carried on working without a break. This put a new perspective on what we in the developed world saw as progress, and it is right that aid workers are now questioning their role.

Back To Work

Pat's test was set, but she hadn't written down the answers. Although I knew some of the answers, I wanted to make sure that I was really fair in marking them. So I went through lots of books to check. I had to then write out the answers in English. The markers of the papers had to be English speakers and writers. There were very few in the camp – Cyprien spoke excellent English, Faustin spoke good English, and Joseph, who was Andre's interpreter, spoke fairly good English. Questions which had to be answered by the health workers were basic – things like naming sexually transmitted diseases and asking for advice that could be given to a person with diarrhoea.

When the health workers left the examination room, they all were saying how easy the examination was. I was beginning to wonder if we had set it at too low a standard and wondered what we would do if everyone got 100%! The maximum mark was ninety-four.

Faustin and Cyprien found a quiet room and in order to be fair, I ensured that whenever they were marking, I was not too far away. When Andre did not need his interpreter, Joseph came too. I checked every paper after they had marked it. Although I didn't understand the language, I could check that the marks were added up properly. I then asked Tharcisse to recheck the questions again to see if he agreed they had been marked fairly. It was a mammoth task and took the best part of a week. The range of marks was between 15 and 78, with three-quarters of the health workers getting between 33% and 66%. I had also had a discussion with Leonard and Celestin, the two supervisors of the health workers. They were going to act as 'referees', and if anyone disagreed with their marks, they would look at the paper and adjust the marks if they thought that this was appropriate. They were also, between them, going to make a list of the practical skills of each health worker, marking them according to their reliability and teaching and communicating skills. We agreed that we would combine the marks. This was not a foolproof system. It was as good as we could get under the circumstances.

On Thursday, when we were nearly complete, Andre came to see me to order me to cancel the test. I asked why, and he said that some of the questions asked things which the health workers had not been taught, and they were being marked by refugees, who could be bribed, and not by a doctor, who would be better at knowing if the answers were right or wrong. I pointed out that they were written in Kinyarwanda, the Rwandan language, not French, and therefore I *had* to use refugees to mark them, but I had tried to make it fair. If any question asked something which had not been taught, then all of the health workers had the same disadvantage. We conducted this conversation with a combination of my poor French and Andre's improving English. It was not easy, and obviously Andre didn't want a translator. I said I would cancel the test if I heard of widespread corruption, but so far I hadn't. Andre eventually saw that he was not going to change my mind and he abruptly got up and left saying, "Okay".

During the week it remained wet, and for us, as soon as we had found a route which was passable to get to work, the lorries churned it up again and our drivers were looking for new routes. I described earlier the deep drains dug along the edge of most roads. They were really needed now. When we travelled along small dirt roads without drains, along the middle of the road the rains had washed a higgledy-piggledy line down the road, with steep sides, looking like a mini grand canyon. Some of these crevices were very deep, and the cars had to take care not to get their wheels trapped in them. This meant that they had to drive carefully and close to the edges of the road. Sometimes the car was at such an angle that you had to hold your breath, wondering if it could keep a grip and not overbalance, even with the four-wheel drive.

The road menders had started work repairing some of the dirt roads on the way to the camp. They ploughed the earth and rolled it again until the surface was level and firm. It was a similar procedure to making tarmac roads, except for a tarmac road, the surface is sprayed with tar afterwards, and, of course, tarmac roads have wider, deeper ditches lined with walls.

Part of the work which I was doing during the week was at the day hospital, where I was trying to write job descriptions, while Faustin and Cyprien marked papers. I had made myself a small office there by rearranging the hospital storage areas. It wasn't entirely satisfactory. There were gaps under the eaves, which provided light, but of course they also let in rain. Depending on which way the wind blew, it could get very wet. Paperwork would get soaked in a few moments. So we had to be alert. There was a waterproof wooden box where I could put papers, and inside I had some plastic carrier bags. So, at the first spot of rain, the desk was cleared of important papers and work had to stop. Sometimes we had to go to Pat's office in MCH. MCH was built of brick, and the window was on the sheltered side, so rain rarely came in.

The auxiliaries in the day hospital were not trained nurses, but the responsibility they took and the technical skills they displayed would only have been performed in England by nurses with extended roles. For example, they set up infusions at the beginning of the day and took them down when the patients went home at four o'clock. They gave all sorts of injections, including intravenous drugs, and gave out tablets and pills. The names of the auxiliaries were Theodosie and Anastase. The other workers were Jean-Baptiste and Gilbert. Gilbert was the cleaner, but most of the cleaning was done before patients came to the hospital each morning. So I taught him how to take and record temperatures, and Jean-Baptiste showed him how to apply compresses. Many of the people who arrived with malaria had temperatures over 40° and they had to be stripped and have cold flannels applied. It worked amazingly well, and often the temperature was down to normal within a few hours. The fifth person who worked in the hospital was Languid, a young Burundian girl, who was meant to keep the paperwork together and escort patients to Kirundo. This escort service could not be done by a refugee as they could not leave the camp. I had decided we needed a qualified nurse in the hospital. The qualified nurse could prescribe, admit and discharge patients. While doing the staff review, I had more or less decided that I would not be able to keep low-paid Burundians such as Languid, because it would cause ill-feeling. The only Burundians I intended to keep were those with particular training or skills, the qualified nurses and managers. If we had a qualified nurse working in the day hospital, then we would not need to send so many patients to Kirundo for treatment, and then we could save money. Having seen the facilities there, I knew that patients were better looked after with us.

The heavy rain was a real trouble to us all. One lunchtime a dispenser left all of the drug pots open while going home for dinner. The door to the dispensing room was locked so that the drugs could not be stolen. On return, all of the pots of tablets were soaked with rainwater following a storm, and we had to throw most of them away. It was an expensive mistake.

At home I had no electricity at all during the week as the generator, always temperamental, had now given up completely. We had had a new generator installed for two days, but when we packed up on evacuation to Kigali it had been dismantled and never came back. There was no gas either, but one guard worked miracles with the barbecue. At the base was a bit of dry grass, which he stored in a plastic bag so that the rain could not wet it. On top was some charcoal. The barbecue had a handle. The grass was lit, and the barbecue swung round in a big circle at a great rate. The fire soon sparked to life and it was ready to put my kettle on to boil.

We had set Saturday morning for Cyprien to write an essay. Fortunately, the rain stayed away. This was for his application for a scholarship for the World University Service placement. After he had written the essay, I had to take it to Kigali to fax it through to David, who would then send it to the World University Service. Emer was coming too as she wanted a break from curfew life and had a friend who worked in Kigali. We were delayed because Padraig and Emer went to a peace conference in Kirundo in the morning. This consisted of local and national politicians talking about why peace was important and included food and traditional singing and dancing. As soon as it had finished, we were on our way.

Kigali And Back

We met a bit of extortion at the border. The border clerk sat in his office wearing a smart set of cream brown-edged pyjamas. He was rather fat and had a smart moustache. He looked at our passports carefully and shook his head. They were valid for multiple *entries* but not multiple *exits*. He had to think about this. While he thought, the office filled with wasps and we had to keep swatting them out of the door. He slowly filled the register with our passport details and names. He smiled a big smile and announced that if we paid a fine of ten dollars each, he could let us out of Burundi. With not much choice we paid up and left.

In Kigali, the weather was glorious. I went to the UN and sent many pages of a fax on a very high-speed machine. Then I returned to the house and waited for David's call to say that it had arrived.

We had to leave some tyres in Kigali and take the generator back to Kirundo. At every checkpoint we were searched, and the soldiers were extremely slow. By the time we got back near to Kirundo it was getting close to curfew. The soldiers at the Burundian checkpoints had already had their share of Primus. They begged for money to buy more. We didn't give them any, but they let us through. We were glad to be back.

An Unexplained Death

On Monday 8th May, Dimitri, a Greek who worked for Catholic Relief Services in Kirundo, was killed. The news reached us by Tuesday morning. I did not know him well but I knew what he looked like. He was last seen alive in his car in Ngosi on Monday lunchtime. His car was found eleven kilometres from Kirundo. His body was found in a side road, tipped out of his car into the middle of the road, and he had been shot.

Catholic Relief Services worked amongst displaced Burundian people in and near Kirundo, and Dimitri was the only expatriate employee. He and his family had lived in Bujumbura for many years. He had recently been involved in reporting people to the authorities who had stolen food from a store and was going to be a witness at their trial. At Maddy's leaving party he spoke to some of the CONCERN team and said that he thought that he had been a target. At the time he was shot, he had been to Bujumbura for wages, was carrying seven million Burundian Francs (400=£1), and he was not travelling in convoy. The Governor of Kirundo thought that he had been killed for simple theft. The UN were not so sure and thought that he might have been assassinated by enemies locally, because of his stand on corruption and theft.

Following the news, of course, we all had a big meeting. We decided that if any rumour was heard that any of our team could be a target for any reason, we would report it and the person would immediately leave for good. We were then all asked if we felt in any way personal targets. I did state that when I made Burundians redundant the following week, the thought had crossed my mind that someone could take it personally. This did not mean that I was losing sleep over it, just that I had considered it as an outside possibility. Naturally, Dimitri's death affected all of us more than other deaths.

He was someone we knew. It also brought home to us just how much we took this volatile, unpredictable country for granted.

Work Progress

One of the strange developments was my relationship with Andre. At work we seemed to get on really well. We talked about things and I made a big attempt to involve him with my work, although usually he said that he would leave it to me.

He was due to leave at the weekend, but because he didn't like saying goodbye, he wanted it to remain a secret. He asked if I would give a present to a friend of his after he left, and I said I would. Things were fine. Yet every time we were in a meeting, Andre would openly disagree with everything I said. I suggested, when we had a quiet talk together one day, that he should bring any problems to me so that we could put them right before meetings. He said of course he would, but he didn't and he carried on as before. It really was how he coped with whatever it was that was annoying him, and I had to accept that. Increasingly, there were some pointers which indicated that there could be a relationship between Andre and Languid, whom I was going to make redundant. I didn't look for evidence, nor did I confront him with it and I never knew whether this was the reason for his hostility or not.

One aspect of my work as health coordinator was dealing with doctors and officials from the United Nations. They visited the camp to discuss refugee health problems, and I found this very informative. One day we had a doctor who specialised in family planning and she came to look at our system. Pat was away and my time was increasingly pressured. I asked Leonard, the supervisor in health education, and Vincent, the technical assistant in MCH, to show her around and tell her how the system in the camp, which was set up by Pat, had been organised. This was an excellent idea. The local staff felt completely involved and they responded superbly to the increased responsibility. The UN official and Leonard talked about the possibility of using the male health workers to distribute condoms throughout the camp. She said that men were more likely to accept condoms if they didn't have to visually appear at a department and give their name. If any were sold on the black market, it didn't really matter who used them, as it would still reduce the population and incidence of VD and Aids.

Another visitor was an entomologist who was interested in our mosquitoes. Again, every day was hectic, so I involved Jim the engineer to escort him to look at the *blundes*. Apparently, what happened was that the *blundes* in various places were sealed up, a plastic sheet was put on the floor, and the inside of the blunde was sprayed with insect killer. We reached a world record of forty mosquitoes. We were assured that the highest earlier record was sixteen. The offending insects were then taken away to be tested for the malarial parasite. Where there is water, the numbers of mosquitoes increase. Where there are big collections of people, then the percentage of malaria-carrying insects increases as disease is spread from one person to another. I left the camp before I was able to find out the results of the tests. If there was a very high concentration of malaria-carrying insects, the area could be with sprayed with insecticide.

We also had frequent visits and discussions with UN doctors concerning our TB patients. Normally WHO would only release drugs for TB sufferers following three positive sputum tests. We had half-treated sufferers, some of whom had undergone tests in Kirundo, which we assumed to be positive as treatment had commenced, and some who had never had a test but to whom Kirundo doctors had commenced treatment following a diagnosis based on symptoms. We had an administrative problem – our patients had been treated for long enough to have negative results from any sputum test and therefore they didn't qualify for treatment. Yet without treatment, they could become ill again. To get over this hurdle meant many radio calls to Anne in Bujumbura and several discussions with UN doctors. Eventually, we had some drugs delivered to us. The next problem was finding out who was in need of treatment. We had no records, as we hadn't treated people in the past. Some people came to the clinic every day and chased me for medication, and these were easy to find. Other people couldn't be bothered to continue with treatment, but finding them and treating them was just as important, as without treatment the disease could spread through the camp. Here we used the health workers again and we were beginning to forge useful links.

We also had a problem of where to put the TB patients. At first they were housed in a room at the rear of the day hospital. The staff from the dysentery unit provided them with their food. This was not ideal, especially as it could cause cross-infection. After negotiations with Charles, the manager of therapeutic feeding, and Reverien, the manager of the dysentery unit, we planned alterations so that part of the Therapeutic Unit could be adapted to a six-bed ward for TB sufferers.

The big work now was the staff review, which meant that I worked from 6.30 a.m. to 11 p.m. everyday, as I had to continue with Pat's work on staffing levels as well as my own while she was in Rwanda. The more I had to do, the happier I felt. I like working under pressure. I gave myself one evening off on Thursday. I went to the Top House with a video of my daughter's wedding. They had electricity and television. Everyone had gone to the bar for a drink. From 6 p.m. to 9 p.m. I watched the video, time after time, watching the faces of my lovely family and friends. This was a real treat for me.

Kirundo hospital had no surgeon, as the Russian doctor had left. Andre was the only doctor in Kirundo. He was called away to do a few operations in the hospital, which he really enjoyed. One day Jim and I were on the way back to Kirundo, and a pregnant lady who was in the last stages of labour and bleeding was put into the car by a midwife from MCH. Andre was in the operating theatre performing a caesarean on an earlier admission. The lady in the car with us was getting more and more desperate as the birth became imminent. When we got to the hospital, we loaded her rapidly on the trolley and rushed her into the hospital. As she arrived in the operating theatre a baby girl popped out into the world. Mother and daughter were both well and neither were in need of any more medical attention. It was the first birth I had attended for well over twenty years. Witnessing the arrival of a new life is always a wonderful privilege.

Leaving

By Wednesday, the NGO in Ngosi had decided that they would protest for a week by not working, to demonstrate that they considered the taking of Dimitri's life was unacceptable to them. Andre, while in the hospital, heard people say that if the white people in Burundi were not doing anything for the people, they might as well be killed. Dublin would take no chances. At five o'clock on Friday we heard that we were to leave Burundi on Sunday morning. For me, this meant that my last two weeks in the camp, when I had planned to say farewell to everyone and hand over responsibilities gradually, were to be pushed into two hours.

There was so much to do. On Saturday morning I had to arrive at the camp with a pile of redundancy notices in my hand and give them out. I couldn't see everyone personally. I had to give a pile to Faustin in MCH, a pile to Charles in Therapeutic, a pile to Leonard in Health Education, and I took responsibility for seeing everyone in the clinic and hospital myself. It was not the sort of task which I would have chosen for my last day. Instead of happy memories, I left people feeling devastated at the loss of their income, knowing that they could not get any other job easily. In addition, I had to once again ensure that there were two week supply of everything in the camp. At least I'd had a practice run when we'd done the previous evacuation.

Saturday was a national holiday known as 'The Day of the Nurse'. There was a small celebration party in the hospital. Everyone I knew well from the camp was in there. So I went and announced that I would not be returning after the evacuation.

By the afternoon Rob had arrived, and at a meeting with all of the Burundian staff in Kirundo he told them why we had to go away for two weeks. At the time, as always, we were not sure whether a team would return. This time the target seemed to be us, as the civil unrest seemed to have settled down in Burundi for the time being.

This was a real break up of the team. Jim and Meduoc were still with us, but the plan had been for them both to transfer to Tanzania during the following week, so they would not return. Andre's contract had ended and this would have been his last day anyway. And I was due to leave in two weeks, so I would not return either. Only Padraig and Emer were planning to return. We had a party in the evening at Top House, ate, drank, and played silly games, before packing up and loading everything into the cars yet again on Sunday morning. It was raining heavily as we left. The road to Kigali was dirt track and slippery. We had a convoy of four cars and I travelled with Meduoc. We were processed at the border in one and a half hours, and while we were there the sun came out. We got to Kigali by mid-afternoon.

I moved my flight forward by a week and spent the time in Kigali on a computer, writing out reports so that the person who followed would know what we had achieved in healthcare at the camp and what we had planned to do next. I couldn't hand over to Pat – she had gone to Zimbabwe on holiday and flew straight back to Goma in Zaire, where she was covering for a nurse who had gone off sick with malaria. I spoke to her on the radio and she was fine. I returned to England on 22nd May and was met by a happy and relieved David at Heathrow airport. The next time I go overseas, we plan to go together.

I was amazed at how easily I settled down. It was almost as if I had only been away for a short holiday. England and Africa are like two different worlds. You can't really compare what I had and what they had.

The main shock was realising how much we waste. In Africa, there was no waste. When I said this to friends and family, sometimes they sounded as if they knew what I meant and then they would say "I recycle everything too", or "What do they do with their vegetable peelings?" People who have always lived in our world can't understand what 'no waste' means. It means wearing your one set of clothes until it falls to bits, and then using the bits left for cleaning cloths, wrapping your baby, or anything else you can think of. It means washing your clothes in the river without detergent, by scrubbing them and leaving them to bleach in the sun. It means using a carrier bag which you were lucky to have found in the road two years ago to store all of your belongings in so that they don't get wet.

It means finding a use for every bit of food that you grow or buy, including bones and skin. It means never seeing, touching, or knowing about packaging materials. It means digging your own latrine in your yard. It means fetching a large can of water from the nearby lake and making it last all day. It means never in your life buying a machine which makes your life easier or more amusing, and never having to dispose of a machine that wears out. It means going to bed when it gets dark and never putting on an electric light or even an oil lamp. It means never buying a newspaper or book. It means never catching a bus or train and never riding in a car.

To throw away plastic bottles, cardboard boxes, and newspapers, which I knew would be a precious commodity in Africa, suddenly seemed to show me how different our worlds are. My life has been enriched by the opportunity I have had to compare.

Reflections

This was my life's ambition, my longed-for exciting adventure. Before I left, a friend said that I would return "cured or worse". This was my first experience of work in an underdeveloped country. I hope it won't be my last. Life was frustrating, perplexing, complicated, lonely, stimulating, challenging, exhilarating, exciting, and it gave me everything I had hoped for. I went knowing that there would be times when I would sometimes be unhappy and sometimes homesick, and I was. I never expected otherwise. I went *for me*. There was nothing for anyone else. Any good which I did in Africa was just the price I paid for pleasing myself. My family and friends know what I did was a purely selfish act. Part of the selfishness was leaving them behind to follow my dream.

I learned an immense amount about Africa, aid work, and tropical diseases. I found I had a different set of skills to most of the people I met, because of my business background. Most useful of all, I found that I could adapt to the environment and adapt my previous managerial experience and skill to the new environment – I *could* do it. At a personal level, my own experience showed me that aid agencies make up their mind before they listen to their employees. Some critics feel that they do not listen to the people to whom they deliver aid. Instead, they truly listen to their sponsors. The sponsors are, in a sense, the customers, and so in some ways this relationship between sponsor and agency is natural and understandable. But staff are the lifeblood of the organisation and listening and hearing what staff say can make an organisation more efficient, stable, robust, and dynamic. This was the only certain conclusion which I drew. The rest of my conclusions were questions not answers.

I hoped when I was there that I would be able to look dispassionately at the situation and observe whether what I did and what others did was worthwhile. I did observe, and from that I drew my own conclusions. What I have written is my personal view. There is no reason to suppose that my personal view is the right one. It is just my own perspective on life while delivering aid to Africa.

When I was in Africa, I read some books which were very critical of the work of aid agencies. A common criticism is the use of aid to prop up corrupt regimes. I also read that by imposing European education on African children we were taking away the opportunity for children to find out what they need to learn from their fathers. Important information like how to farm a barren farmland in order to get enough off it for a family to survive. These skills in Africa might be just as important as computer skills in Britain. But by taking children away from their apprenticeship in farming skills so that they can learn how to write, they end up having to move to shanty towns surrounding a city, scratching a living by doing menial work. And if land is not farmed properly, then the population may starve and end up needing food aid. Can we look back with certainty and say that our intervention has made it *better*? Could a more appropriate education include technical skills to build on local knowledge which would give much needed opportunities to develop agriculture? And yet a black boy in South Africa had a European-style education and grew up to be a great and respected leader. Without education, could he have been the same man, and would South Africa have peacefully moved to majority rule? It is this sort of question which as yet has no answer. Perhaps we'll be able to look back after generations have passed and truly evaluate the outcome of the work which is being done now.

I learned a great deal, but the most striking thing I learned was that we *didn't* know and *couldn't* know whether what we are doing is right. I also learned that knowing that there was no answer was no excuse for not asking the question.

I went to Africa at a time when agencies were changing their nature and increasing their political influence. I went from an aggressively competitive business environment in England to a new and rapidly developing aid industry, as yet with no real business goals. Doing accounts means that you monitor income and expenditure. Preparing budgets means that you have parameters for spending. All of this seems to happen. But, as yet, there appears to be to be no real market economy, no real financial accountability to sponsors and donors. Inevitably, I feel that just as the market mentality has reached the health care services in our world, it will reach African Aid too.

When I went to Africa, I knew so little that I could not set personal goals before I got there. I knew there would be a challenge – I didn't know what it was. I had heard that there was corruption, and the presence of personnel such as myself from donor countries was to control and supervise the distribution of aid. This, in effect, is a difficult thing to do in a place with no effective judiciary. For example, you can catch 'small fry' – the cleaner who steals hospital food, the food distributor who creams off some oil to sell in the market. He or she can soon be sacked. But big scale corruption is a different thing to tackle. One of CONCERN's senior managers was a friend of influential people in Kirundo province. It was strongly felt that he falsely claimed huge sums of money after pretending that latrines had been dug when they hadn't. It was investigated and evidence was found. The culprit didn't even have a warning letter. Was this right? Perhaps so. If he had been dismissed, then perhaps an employee of CONCERN would have had the same fate as Dimitri. But then, if we have to tolerate corruption in order to safeguard our lives, perhaps the question we should ask is simply, should we be there at all?

There is no doubt that with our presence, the refugees in the camp were safer. In Burundi the total Hutu population is at the mercy of the Tutsi extremists, just as in Rwanda, the Tutsi population is at the mercy of Hutu extremists. But are we protecting people who should in fact be held responsible for killing many of their fellow men? But if they were incited, driven, fed false information, and led to believe that they must kill others or be killed themselves, are they perpetrators or victims? And without an effective system for finding out the truth and dispensing a real justice, should we be trying to influence Rwanda to think of modifying its goals – to search for and punish only the leaders, and to show compassion to the followers?

The experience of Kibeho showed that when camps are dispersed, people return home and regain their independence. There are hundreds of thousands of Rwandan refugees, all dependent on handouts from the developed world. The lesson refugees learn is how to be dependent. Some of the facilities which are provided, such as health care, are more accessible and better in a refugee camp than provisions which the population would expect to get at home. This makes leaving the camp a more difficult decision for any potential returnees. There are pressures to make them want to stay, one of which is a fear of returning to a situation of ethnic violence. That fear is stoked up by the *interahamwe*, the Hutu militia, who want the camps to remain where they are for their own political reasons. Aid agencies which run camps well and efficiently, protecting, employing, training and befriending refugees, may in themselves be perpetuating the cycle of dependency. If an aid agency is good at its job, perversely, it reduces the will of the population it serves from reaching out for independence.

Should we give aid at all? There *is* a case for leaving Africa to its own devices. By being there, guarding, protecting, taking control, being benefactors, we prevent Africans from gaining confidence in their own abilities and feeling pride in their own heritage. Should we learn to look at the ill-equipped, dirty and poorly-organised western-style hospitals and schools and listen to evidence of corruption with interest only? If we truly left Africa to itself, could it learn to take control effectively in an African way? There would initially be continent chaos, with disease, death, and civil war. From this could a truly great nation arise with its own solutions and self-pride? Would it be moral for the world to wait and watch as a continent destroyed its human contents before starting to build itself again? On the 8th April 1995 in *The Economist* it was reported that the World Food Programme (WPF) USAID and UNICEF all admitted that they themselves were a cause of the conflict in Burundi. Aid was manipulated so that governments could keep up bickering, instead of getting on with the job of running their countries. This could be true of all countries which receive aid or any outside assistance.

What about the morals of the aid agencies? They are big business now. Working your way up the ladder of an aid agency can lead you to good job prospects. Yet aid is mostly given on the backs of disaster and conflict. Is it right that some individuals should prosper because of the misfortune of others? Or should it be that individuals are encouraged to develop skills and experience so that they can set up coping mechanisms in emergency situations, and in order to encourage m to do so, is it only right that they should be paid sufficient to rd their expertise? Often, relatively young people in places like da hold positions of power and authority which they could not te in the developed world. For example, a nurse in England would not be responsible for two hundred employees without considerable experience and managerial qualifications. In Africa, a simple registered nurse qualification gained in Britain and a couple of years experience working in a camp could put an employee in that situation. Is that fair to them? Can they do justice to the job? I went to Burundi mainly to enjoy being there. Like me, many young and newly qualified people went to Rwanda and Burundi to have a good time, and I don't personally object to that at all, though others might. I saw excesses: heavy drinking and smoking, casual sexual encounters. That was the way in which they coped with the stresses of living in a completely different and sometimes dangerous and lonely world. The people who work for aid agencies have unusual pressures, a different sort of life, and they are a long way from the restraints that still exist even in our liberated society. Should they be more controlled ambassadors for their country, or is it acceptable for them too to show their human weaknesses?

People who work for aid agencies often don't have to take any responsibility for things which at home are part of the pressures of ordinary living. For example, accommodation is provided, food is paid for, transport is provided, and alcohol is often free. When people don't have to think about these things, then they take advantage of the situation, and it can end up giving the Third World a distorted impression of our society. For example, one day we were invited to a party, two hours drive from Kigali. Four personnel travelled there in three cars, and two drivers were paid for the journey. Drivers were also paid an overnight allowance, and they stayed two nights. They could have taken one or two cars and stayed one night and still attended the same party. The cost reduction would have been considerable. But if it is not your own money, no one economises – that's human nature. Aid workers may have considered this a justifiable form of remuneration for working as a volunteer or for a very low salary. But some donor paid for these expenses, either a country which raised money by taxes or an individual who was moved with compassion. If the aid agencies have to move towards a market economy, will these sorts of expenses be put under scrutiny? And should aid workers be made to think about the impression they are creating to the African? Or is it unreasonable to expect aid workers to be paragons of virtue and should they be prepared to accept the life standards of the indigenous population in addition to the other stresses of the job?

I am certainly not implying in any way that my agency, CONCERN, was any less caring, efficient or moral than any other agency. Most of the people I met and worked with impressed me with their abilities, personal characteristics, and dedication to their work. The point in my reflections is that I found no answers, but only questions to ponder on. The next time the world witnesses a tragedy and it is reported on the television news, I shall still look with compassion and understand that the victims are human and cannot be ignored simply because they were born on a different continent. I shall still think that something must be done. I now have a little insight into the complexities which exist. What I know is that I have seen enough to know that I have a lot more to learn. What I want, is to help other people to think as well, so that many heads can reflect on the same questions, and we may then be nearer to an answer.

I returned to England, and on my first day I heard a snippet of news: 87% of companies in Britain have been victims of fraud by their employees. A friend of mine had changed jobs while I was away. She now works in a council run home and has discovered a huge wages fraud. When she told her immediate superior, she was warned not to talk about the problem she had uncovered. If the unions became involved in the event that irregularities were exposed, then her own position would be extremely difficult.

Corruption and crime are not exclusive to Africa. We are only human too.

Follow Up

Pat returned to England where we had a happy reunion. She spent the summer fund-raising for CONCERN, visiting sponsors in Austria and Germany, while waiting for further postings overseas.

Via the World University Service, Cyprien was offered a place at Staffordshire University to take a degree in Development Studies and Management. After several months, he managed to get an exit visa from Burundi agreed in principle. He is hoping to take up his place in September 1996.

David and I are taking Master's degrees in Development, Planning and Administration, and following this we hope to find work together overseas.

CONCERN finally left the project in Ruku camp, Kirundo, in the summer of 1995, due to operational difficulties which were encountered in Burundi. An African Aid agency took over the management of the project in Kirundo – the camp is still there. CONCERN continues to work in Rwanda, where an important part of their work is supporting people who wish to return to their original homes, and tracing families of displaced children.

Bibliography

AFP, 'Tutsi and Hutu Clash in Burundi', *The Daily Telegraph*, 25.3.95.

African Rights, *Rwanda, Death, Despair and Defiance*, (2nd Edition) African Rights, London, 1995.

African Rights, *Rwanda – Who is Killing, Who is Dying*, African Rights, London, 1994.

African Rights, *Humanitarianism Unbound?*, African Rights, London, 1994.

CONCERN WORLDWIDE, *Crisis in Central Africa*, CONCERN, Dublin, undated.

Dowden, R, 'UN Helpless as Fears of Burundi Genocide Grow', *The Independent*, 28.3.95.

Economist Intelligence Unit, *Economist Intelligence Unit Country Profile 1994/5 Rwanda and Burundi*: London, 1995.

Economist Editorial, 'Burundi on the Brink', *The Economist* 8.4.95.

Independent (Reuter report), 'Burundi Killings Reported at 150', *The Independent*, 27.3.95.

Kiley, S, 'Burundi Murder Raises Tension', *The Times*, 13.3.95.

McGreal, C, 'Burundi Buries Hopes of Peace,' *The Guardian*, 17.3.95.

McGreal, C, 'Burundi's Demographic Time Bomb Ticks Louder than Ever', *The Guardian*, 21.3.95.

Orr, D, 'Burundi on the Brink of an Orgy of Killing', *The Independent*, 23.5.95.

Orr, D, 'Burundi Hutus Flee Cleansing by Tutsis', *The Independent*, 31.3.95.

Orr, D, 'Report from Kibeho Camp, Rwanda', *The Independent*, 28.4.95.

Regional Survey of the World, *Africa South of the Sahara*, 24th edition, Europa Publications, Rochester, 1995.

Tunbridge, L, 'Fear of New Refugee Crisis as Panic Sweeps Burundi', *The Daily Telegraph*, 31.3.95.

Vassal-Adams, G, *Rwanda, an Agenda for International Action*, Oxfam, Oxford, 1994.

Glossary

BF	Burundian Francs
EC	European Community
Frodebu	Front pour la Democratie au Burundi
MCH	Maternal and Child Health Department
MSF	Medecins Sans Frontiers
NGO	Non-Governmental Organisation
OAU	Organisation of African Unity
PDC	Partie Democratique Chretien
RPA	Rwandan Patriotic Army
RPF	Rwandan Patriotic Front
UN	United Nations
UNAMIR	United Nations Assistance Mission to Rwanda
UNHCR	United Nations High Commission for Refugees
UPRONA	Union Pour le Progress National
VSO	Voluntary Service Overseas
WHO	World Health Organisation